Costume Reference 9

1939-1950

MARION SICHEL

B T Batsford Limited   London

First published 1979
© Marion Sichel 1979
Reprinted 1983, 1985, 1987

ISBN 0 7134 1507 X

Printed and bound in Great Britain by
Anchor Brendon Limited, Tiptree, Essex
for the Publishers B T Batsford Limited,
4 Fitzhardinge Street, London W1H 0AH

Contents

5   Introduction

9   Men
27   Women
64   Children

65   Glossary
70   Select Bibliography
71   Index

Introduction

Sailor and naval officer, 1939-45

This short period in fashion history starts with the Second World War which had such restricting influences, and ends with the fashion revolution of 1947 with Christian Dior's 'New Look'.

Restraint and practicability were the main features of clothing during the War. There was a great deal of uniformity and austerity and 'make do and mend' was the motto. Most young men were in uniform and many women joined the auxiliary forces and were also seen in blue, green and khaki, having joined the WRAF, WRENS and ATS . Those who did not join the Armed Forces, but were in civilian occupations, were restricted by many shortages. From June 1941 clothes rationing on coupons restricted the amount of cloth used in clothing and men's suits suffered as much as women's clothes.

Siren suits popularized by Winston Churchill, the wartime Prime Minister, were worn by all classes of people. These suits, extremely comfortable and convenient, were a great social equaliser, and also seemed to give all who wore them a protected feeling. They were all-in-one suits which could be worn over almost any garment, and they zipped all the way up the front. Attached hoods made them extra warm for wear in air raid shelters at night. These suits, originally designed for wartime use, evolved later into fashionable hostess wear.

As the Government had decreed certain restrictions on the use of materials, a standard was set with utility clothing, and all clothing that was up to the required standard was stamped

CC41. This was approved by the Board of Trade and the fashion trade cooperated in keeping to the standard.

Men's suits generally became single-breasted and the amount of pockets reduced to a maximum of five. Waistcoats were rarely seen and trouser turn-ups also disappeared. Men's fashions were mainly replaced by service uniforms during the War, but in the late 1940s 'dandies' again made their appearance. These were the 'Teddy Boys' who brought back the fashions of the Edwardian era, but tried to look tough at the same time. The padded shoulders of their jackets (called drapes) were accentuated and their trousers became very narrow, and were known as drainpipes.

Men's trendy clothes with the 'American' look were introduced after the War in 1946, and included double-breasted jackets with wide shoulders, large lapels and big drapes. Shirts often had long pointed collars and ties often had hand-painted pictures down the front.

The general silhouette of women during the War years was quite plain and square. Jackets and coats had padded shoulders to give a severe outline, and even dresses and blouses followed this mode, whilst skirts were straight and narrow. To give the appearance of extra fullness, many skirts were cut on the cross or bias. Pleats and pockets as well as other trimmings were seldom seen. Even unnecessary buttons were omitted, and only labour saving methods were allowed, thus elaborate stitching and embroidery was omitted from bought clothes.

A practical wartime fashion that gradually replaced the wearing of ladies' hats was the turban which was first worn in factories as safety attire to keep long hair from getting entangled in machinery. Turbans were later worn as fashionable headdress as well as in food shops for hygienic reasons.

Stockings, very hard to get, and also extremely expensive, were often replaced by the painting of the legs in a tan colour with a seam drawn down the back with eyebrow pencil. Socks were also worn by many.

Shoes were also made to be hardwearing rather than fashionable, and were quite clumsy in appearance.

However, people did often manage to contrive quite good effects with what they did have. With inventiveness and imagination non-coupon items such as blankets could be turned into coats, whilst pillow slips and sheets could be made into summer dresses and blouses. Old clothes were also converted into new ones by alterations and sometimes by making one new garment out of, maybe, two old ones.

WAAF War uniform and ATS uniform

RAF sergeant, 1939-45

The three girls are in naval dress. The one on the left is in a mess gown of the 1950s, the centre one in a suit c. 1942 and the one on the right in an overcoat c. 1939

In 1942 the Incorporated Society of London Fashion Designers was formed but they designed almost only for the export market, whilst mass-produced clothes had to suffice for Great Britain.

In 1946 the Council for Industrial Design staged an exhibition called 'Britain can Make it' at the Victoria and Albert Museum. This gave British dress and fabric designers a chance to show off their new post-war designs, but, again, unfortunately most items were for export only.

In 1947, Christian Dior launched his 'New Look' which at first was not approved of, but nevertheless soon captivated the world. The skirts were full and to mid-calf, with tiny wasp waists, and the bodices had soft sloping shoulders. The evening dresses that he designed were very often strapless. The full skirts were often padded at the hips and the bosoms were rounded. Long dolman sleeves were also popular as they also helped to emphasize the small waists.(As fabric shortages still existed, in practice, many skirts were lengthened by either inserting or adding a contrasting material to the hems.)

In this era, from the outbreak of the Second World War to the 'New Look' of 1947, the whole fashion industry changed over on a massive scale to mass-produced clothes, both men's and women's fashions being sold in chain stores as well as specialist shops. Fashionable men's suits had previously been designed and made to measure only in Savile Row, the men's equivalent to the Haute Couture scene, but the quality of mass-produced off-the-peg suits had so risen that they had virtually taken over the market. The same was true for mass-produced ladies' wear, which also reached very high standards during this period. Further advances in fashion were made possible by the new range of synthetic fabrics, primarily nylon, which encouraged many designers to explore the potential of other man-made fibres.

Air Force officer, 1939-45

Christian Dior's 'New Look'; close-fitting waisted jacket, full skirt and wide coolie-type straw hat, c. 1947

Men

The Second World War brought austerity and clothes rationing so that men who were not in the Armed Forces were governed in their buying of new clothes by the number of coupons they had. Only the most essential items of clothing could be bought: a utility suit used up almost half a year's supply of coupons, for instance. This brought about a decline in the standard of dressing, particularly as regards the habit of wearing different outfits for day wear and for the evening or semi-formal occasions, a custom that never returned. If, however, formal dress was required, it was always possible to hire the complete outfit including shirts, ties and shoes.

'Make do and mend', a wartime slogan, had also invaded the male clothing trade. Repairing and turning services were to be seen everywhere.

Civil Defence organisations such as the ARP (Air Raid Precautions) and AFS (Auxiliary Fire Service) had their own uniform that consisted of a dark blue combination or siren suit with patch pockets and also pockets at the side of the trouser legs. The badge of the particular service was displayed above one of the breast patch pockets. Battle dress was also sometimes worn in dark blue. Steel helmets were also an essential part of the uniform as was the carrying of gas masks.

During the War years two-piece lounge suits, without waistcoats, were mainly worn, and this fashion remained popular, even after the War, especially in the warm summer months. Lounge and sports jackets, influenced by American Service styles, often had pleated backs, and wider draped shoulders. By about 1948 these fashions had established themselves, but were being superseded by the Edwardian look with narrower jackets and trousers.

Land Defence Volunteer, 1940

After the War surplus Government and Service clothing came on the market which later influenced fashions. The Army battledress was especially popular as casual wear.

With the advent of man-made fibres, suiting materials became lighter in weight, and shirts were also made in non-iron nylon materials.

FROCK AND MORNING COATS

Frock coats were no longer worn, except for Levy dress and for special occasions such as funerals, and then mainly by the older men. Frock coat styles did not alter. They were mainly double-breasted with three buttons either side. Button stands were present and the lapels also had a buttonhole on each side. Lapels were faced in silk and were either high or of the roll kind to the waistline. Frock coats had a centre back vent with back pleats which had concealed pockets. There were also buttons either side of the centre vent at hip level.

Frock coat sleeves were generally quite plain but could be cuffed. The front edges and cuffs could be trimmed with a flat braid. The coats were generally worn open and the waistcoats worn with frock coats were commonly double-breasted, sometimes with lapels or collars. They were often of the same colour, which was black or grey, as the coat, but they could be a lighter shade. The trousers were mainly striped in grey or could be of black and white checked material.

Morning coats were only worn for weddings and formal occasions such as Garden Parties. They were always worn with grey waistcoats and striped trousers. Morning coats were generally single-breasted with a waist seam, the fronts curving back. The vents at the centre back reached the waist. These coats are also known as tail coats. There were buttons either side of the back vent at the pleats. The sleeves usually had slit cuffs with buttons.

As these outfits were so seldom worn it became customary to hire them. The usual colour of morning coats was grey, and when worn for weddings etc, the top hats to go with them were grey also.

LOUNGE SUITS

Formal clothes had gone into decline and been replaced by more informal wear. The most usual apparel in men's wear was the lounge suit. Lounge suits were worn on most of the occasions for which morning or frock coats had in previous years been essential.

Infantry officer, 1942 and infantry soldier, 1940

The man on the left is in a double-breasted lounge suit with the popular short hairstyle, c. 1941, while the man on the right is wearing a single-breasted suit and trousers without turn-ups, c. 1950. The centre figure is in a soldier's wartime combat dress, c. 1942-45

Lounge suits could include waistcoats, but were sometimes worn with pullovers. For weekend wear the trousers and jackets of the suits could be in different shades. Matching waistcoats finally became unfashionable about 1941, when shortages of materials necessitated restrictions, and the mode for two piece suits remained for a long time.

As lounge suits replaced frock and morning coats, it was fashionable to own black lounge suits.

Jacket styles did not vary a great deal from the previous period. They could be single- or double-breasted and had hip pockets, two breast pockets inside and an inside ticket pocket at hip level. There were generally three buttons at the slit cuffs. Waistcoats, when worn, were generally single-breasted, with two pockets either side, one at the breast, and another at the base. They were usually welted. Trousers often had side pockets in the seams, and hip pockets were also occasionally present. With wartime shortages, the back trouser hip pockets were often dispensed with, as were turn-ups.

The effect of material shortages also became evident about 1941 when jackets became shorter, just reaching the hips, but ending above the crotch. There were also fewer pockets in evidence, and the breast pockets, as well as the flaps on the side pockets were completely removed. Cuff buttons were also not seen any more, thus saving even more on materials.

About 1942 squared shoulders and a draped effect became more common, and a somewhat standard or utility lounge suit evolved. Lounge suits generally closed with three buttons. Double-breasted jackets were no longer made during the War, and this also served to standardize styles.

After the War, in 1945, jackets were made less skimpy and slightly draped, they were looser fitting over the chest, and the shoulder line became less squared and more natural looking. The waistline was also lowered slightly. The more formal lounge suits in black or other sombre colours were seen less after the War, when formality became less important.

This looser and more casual appearance remained, and lounge jackets became more popular for leisure wear as well. Double-breasted jacket styles again became popular after the War when restrictions on the use of materials were lifted.

The American influence, in 1946, made wide shoulders and draped double-breasted jackets very fashionable. In the most extreme style the shoulders were padded to exaggeration and the long styled body was worn mainly by 'spivs', who were men who sold goods on the Black Market, which was

Austerity suit c. 1941

*Centre soldier in battledress blouse and beret of the British army 1946.
The girl on the left is in a New Look outfit with the short-sleeved
jacket with a peplum at the back to give a bustle effect. The small pillbox hat is decorated with net, c. 1949. The man on the right is in a
double-breasted suit and waistcoat, c. 1948*

thriving due to shortages in most commodities. Long rolling lapels were part of the American look, although lapels had in general again become larger since the War and its restrictions.

Servicemen, when they left the Armed Forces, were all issued with a 'demob' (demobilization) suit. These suits were very unenterprising in style, but were reasonably well made, and although the material was economically used, they differed from the wartime utility suits in that the side pockets again had flaps and the jackets could be single- or double-breasted.

Top breast pockets with welts were also seen again, as well as three buttons on the slit sleeve cuffs. The double-breasted demob jackets usually had six buttons and broad roll lapels, which had buttonholes either side to hold flowers if wanted. Inside breast pockets were again available and ticket pockets were usually placed inside the right outside hip pocket. Trousers again had turn-ups and could have three pockets.

About 1949 it became fashionable for the younger generation to wear Edwardian style dress. The jackets were longer and narrower in cut and single-breasted with short lapels. The collars were always faced in velvet. The trousers worn by these 'Teddy Boys' were very narrow and known as 'drain-pipes'.

For summer wear it was generally fashionable to wear grey flannel suits and the jackets could be unlined.

WAISTCOATS

Waistcoats when worn with frock coats were generally double-breasted although occasionally single-breasted styles were seen. They generally had lapels and collars and were of the same colour as the jackets. For wear with morning coats they were generally light grey or black or even a fawn colour, the lighter colours mainly being worn for weddings. Double-breasted styles were the trend, but in general single-breasted waistcoats were more popular. They had five to six buttons, and were usually worn with the bottom button left open.

For summer wear waistcoats were seldom seen, especially during the War when the scarcity of material necessitated economies.

Before the War waistcoats generally had four pockets, but these were reduced to two on the waistcoats made during the War years. A strap and buckle at the back to ensure a better fit was customary and backs of waistcoats were always made of a cheaper lining material, whilst the fronts were of a similar or matching material to the jackets.

Edwardian style dress

14

By about 1950 coloured and patterned material waistcoats appeared. Often they were made of a brocade front and cotton or silk back. For sports wear soft leather waistcoats that had zip fasteners instead of the more conventional buttons also began to be worn.

LEGWEAR

Trousers worn with morning or frock coats were invariably of a black and grey striped material and were without turn-ups. When lounge jackets were worn formally with waistcoats, the trousers were also of a striped, usually cashmere, material and could have turn-ups.

During the early War years false turn-ups on trousers replaced real ones so as to save on material, but by about 1943 even these were no longer to be seen, although later they again became popular.

Just before the War the width of trouser legs was about 58cm at the knees, decreasing to 53cm at the bottom, but in the early 1940s they became narrower, shrinking to about 50cm and 45cm for economy's sake. After the War the legs again became wider, with the trousers slightly longer and breaking well over the shoes.

Towards the end of the 1940s when the Edwardian look became fashionable, trousers became much narrower towards the bottoms and were known as 'peg tops' or 'drainpipes'. Trouser pockets which were in the side seams and were vertical were gradually, after 1945, omitted, and cross pockets, which were towards the front below the waistband, became more fashionable as it was assumed that they were more practical for access when seated in cars. These pockets were placed almost horizontally with the openings sloped. Small fob pockets in the front which had been excluded during the War, were occasionally replaced with a buttoned flap. The back hip pockets, one either side, also usually with buttoned flaps, were replaced after the War, although sometimes only one was present.

Zip fasteners replaced buttons on the flies, and the waistband extended over the centre on one side and fastened with either a hook and bar or button and buttonholes. Adjustable straps, usually one each side of the centre back seam with the elasticated part concealed in the waistband, had the extended material with one or two buttonholes attached to buttons on the waistband. Loops of the same material as the trousers were attached on the waistband at intervals to hold or support a leather or fabric belt.

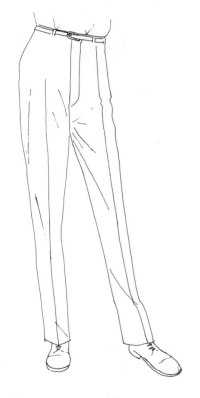

Narrow trousers without turn-ups c. 1944

Soft shirt collars were general, the stiffer detachable collars going out of fashion in the early 1940s. Collars were usually of the same colour as the shirts themselves, or could be white if the shirts were of a patterned material. Shaped celluloid stiffeners were generally inserted in special pockets under the collar points of a soft collar and could be removed for washing. Later, a special material was used to give the collar points a semi-stiff finish. Collar points became longer over the years and a popular fashion for really long points came from the United States.

Shirts with soft collars were also fashionable for wear with dinner jackets.

Long ties with square or, more usually, pointed ends were generally worn. They were mainly made of artificial or real silk, wool or poplin. By the end of the War woollen ties that did not crumple were usually worn with casual clothes.

In the early 1940s spots, checks and stripes were all fashionable for ties, but by the end of the 1940s squares and diamond shaped designs also appeared. By 1950 paisley patterns as well as small floral motifs were included in the many differing patterns available. The American influence, after the War, was also seen in the vivid and bolder prints on the market.

Ready-made ties which fastened at the back with adjustable straps were less popular, but bow ties fastening in the same manner were still available, especially for evening wear.

Wide Ascot ties were mainly worn with morning coats. These consisted of a long scarf or tie which usually had square ends, and these were tied with the ends overlapping at an angle instead of one covering the other, and fastened with an ornamental tie-pin. Ordinary four-in-hand ties could also be worn with morning coats if the shirt collars were of the wing or stand-fall variety.

OUTDOOR WEAR

Chesterfields, popular from the start of the century, still remained the most popular of outdoor coats. They could be either single- or double-breasted. The single-breasted styles could have fly fastenings, whereas the double-breasted styles usually had six buttons and sometimes a half-belt behind. They generally reached to just below the knees and could be slightly shaped to the waist or just hang straight, being cut in one piece. The coat fronts were sometimes kept close together

Single-breasted Chesterfield coat with fly fastening and flapped pockets, and a bowler hat

16

Trench mackintosh and a soft peaked cap, c. 1945

at the hem with a small button on one side whilst the other side had a tab inside with a buttonhole. Back vents were also sometimes seen.

Chesterfields generally had two flapped pockets, one each side, and a welted breast pocket on the left. The revers were fairly wide and could have button-holes. The coats were usually fully lined with black silk or sateen. The sleeve cuffs could be slit with three or four buttons.

Ulster coats, generally of a warmer material, were mainly double-breasted with either an all round belt or half belted at the back and buttoned at the front. The seam down the centre back could be lapped over. The pockets were often of the patch variety.

Raglan sleeves were very popular for various styles of coats, especially raincoats. Raincoats or mackintoshes called 'macs' were often single-breasted, but had full skirts and were belted. Other styles included the more military look with straps at the shoulders of fitted sleeves. Both set-in sleeves and Raglan sleeves could have tabs around the cuffs which were buttoned to give a tighter fit.

Raincoats were often lined in a check material. They could have vents at the back, especially if they were loose fitting and without a belt. The long back seams might have numerous rows of stitching down. The looser styles which were buttoned down the front, and could have a fly, often had a tab or tongue, with a buttonhole or a button on the opposite side almost at the hem in the front to hold the coat together.

After the War, from about 1946, many raincoats were made of nylon and other man-made materials. Some of these were made to be worn over ordinary greatcoats and could be folded up so small that they could easily be carried in a brief-case.

Duffle coats came into use after the War in 1945. These were short coats originally worn by naval men and were usually dark blue or fawn. Duffles were loose fitting and usually had Raglan sleeves and two large patch pockets. These coats were always unlined and, if the sleeves were set in, had a yoked back. The attached hoods, when not worn over the head, formed a kind of deep collar when pushed down. Duffle coats were fastened with wooden toggles and loops made of rope or hemp.

Many of the duffle coats were surplus Navy coats, although many copies in a thick cloth were made. They often just had large collars instead of the attached hoods. Colours were usually navy, maroon, beige and other subdued shades.

Other overcoats, also mainly in sombre colours as well as camel, could have checked or herringbone designs.

Single-breasted coat with set-in sleeves. The hat is an Eden type with the brim edged in braid, c. 1940

FORMAL AND EVENING WEAR

Dress coats were seen less than in previous periods, although they were still occasionally worn. They were always worn open, although they were cut as though they were double-breasted. The fronts were cut away, sometimes straight and sometimes with points. The long below-the-knee skirts at the back were slit in the centre to the waist. The style of dress coats varied only slightly from that of the earlier part of the century. The fronts became so small that they could barely meet and they just covered the waistcoat. The shoulders were more square and the lapels were cut quite large. Sometimes only the collar or lapels were silk faced. Sleeves were often slit and ended with three to four buttons.

Towards the end of the 1940s it was more usual to wear a dinner jacket than tails. If tails or dress coats were necessary, it was quite usual to hire them for a specific occasion.

A very deep navy or midnight blue material became popular for dinner jackets as it was supposed to appear a deeper black in artificial lighting than the usual black barathea. Dinner jackets were generally double-breasted as the necessity for waistcoats was less. In the early 1940s lapels were wide and pointed, or else the collars could be of the deep shawl variety. Continuous roll collars were also popular.

Double-breasted dinner jackets generally only had two buttons whilst the single-breasted styles had just a single button. All dinner jackets had an outside breast pocket on the left to hold a handkerchief which could be folded to show either one or two points. Many dinner jackets had two hip pockets which could be flapped or jetted. Back vents were not unusual. Many jackets, to give them a better shape, had darts in the front from the breast pocket to the hip pockets. The shape and length of dinner jackets followed the styles of the day lounge suit jackets, being very similar in cut.

Stiff shirt fronts and collars, sometimes made of piqué or marcella and known as boiled shirts, were still to be seen in the early 1940s, although soft collars and shirts became more evident. Black bow ties were always worn with dinner jackets, although white piqué batswing bows were more popular with dress coats.

Waistcoats worn with evening wear could be single- or double-breasted. They were in a white piqué when worn with dress coats, whereas the single-breasted ones worn with dinner jackets were black. The waistcoats were low cut and generally had low rolling collars, and two to four buttons.

In the early 1940s when dinner jackets were mainly double-breasted, waistcoats were left off.

Trousers were either deep blue or black to match the jackets with which they were worn, and they were always without turn-ups. The outside seams had one row of braiding when worn with dinner jackets, but two rows were always present when the trousers belonged to dress coats.

After the War formal dress was rarely seen and dark lounge suits were more popular for dinners and theatre outings, although dinner suits were seen on the rare formal occasions. Dress tail coats were worn mainly by waiters, musicians and for ballroom dancing competitions.

For weddings, morning coats, usually in grey, were worn with striped trousers, a waistcoat and a grey top hat.

Gloves, sticks and spats were no longer seen. It became more general for dark lounge suits to be worn for weddings rather than the more formal morning suits, but both always had a white flower in the lapel buttonhole, and a white handkerchief showing in the breast pocket.

For funerals and mourning most men simply wore lounge suits in dark colours with black ties.

For Court occasions and receptions, Court dress was worn. This consisted of black evening dress coat and trousers usually with waistcoats and bow ties as well as gloves.

INFORMAL AND SPORTS WEAR

For informal wear tweed jackets and grey flannel trousers were extremely popular. The tweed jackets, also known as sports jackets, were made similarly to single-breasted lounge suit jackets with the lapels notched. Dark blue blazers, sometimes single- but mainly double-breasted, with gilt buttons were also worn, in both summer and winter. In the early 1940s sports jackets were sometimes yoked and had a half belt at the back. Jackets with pleated backs, similar to Norfolk jackets, were also popular. Just after the War informal jackets could be draped, with the back cut in one without a centre seam.

For summer wear lightweight materials such as gaberdine

Pork pie hat and a British warmer with patch pockets, c. 1942

and cotton were more used than the heavier tweeds and woollen materials which were reserved for the winter. For summer, jackets were mainly in lighter colours such as fawn or light browns. The flannel trousers, also made in worsted, were made in all shades of grey, the darker shades becoming more fashionable after the War. Also in the post-war years checks and stripes as well as colours other than grey helped brighten up the fashions which had become rather dull during the War. Gaberdine, corduroy and cavalry twill all became popular materials.

Trouser waistbands, usually prolonged on one side, fastened with a button. Sometimes in the earlier period, brace buttons were present inside the waistband. If braces were not worn, and they did become very much less popular, there were loops to hold a belt, sewn on the outside of the waistband. There were very often pockets in the side seams (these were welted) and one hip pocket at the back, which was generally jetted and closed with a loop and button.

Smoking jackets were worn less than previously and were made single- or double-breasted, usually of padded silk or velvet edged with a cord of contrasting colour, or bound with silk. The roll collars and cuffs were generally quilted and the closure was with toggles and frogging across the front.

Machine or hand knitted cardigans and pullovers both with and without sleeves were all worn. Cardigans ended just below waist level and were generally buttoned to the low collarless V front opening. They usually had two patch pockets, one on each side. Cardigans were mainly knitted in plain or cable stitch patterns with ribbed edging at the base, neck and cuffs for a firmer finish.

Pullovers, also with ribbed edgings, could be sleeveless and have V shaped necklines, but were made slightly shorter than cardigans. They were also known as slipovers. Long sleeved pullovers or sweaters had a variety of necklines, from high turtle or roll necks to the lower V shapes. Some pullovers had a zip fastening at the neck to facilitate the wearing of them.

Knitwear was sometimes made in such a way as to be reversible, and a different colour each side, so that the garment could be worn in either colour, thus doubling its usefulness, an opportune feature during the shortages.

Sportswear generally consisted of sports jackets, blazers, windcheaters, flannels (trousers), plus-fours (but not as extreme as previously), and shorts. Casual shirts were made in flannel material, cotton and rayon, with the collars always

Woollen lumber jacket with a fur collar and zipper front, c. 1950

Man's sport boot, c. 1948

attached and sometimes worn open without a tie. They could be of checked or striped designs or in plain colours. After the War, nylon shirts were also popular as they required little or no ironing.

Knitted or suede waistcoats were also popular and towards the end of the 1940s many had suede fronts with the backs in a knitted material. Cardigans were also sometimes made in this manner with sleeves, collar and the button stand down the front, of fabric whilst the front only was of leather.

Windcheaters, also called lumber jackets, were generally made of a thick woollen material such as blanket cloth. They had ribbed and elasticated wrist and waistbands to give a closer fit, but were slightly pouched above the elastication. They were either buttoned or zipped to the neck which was also close fitting.

Headwear was worn less, but caps and soft felt hats were still to be seen in the early 1940s.

Footwear consisted of plimsolls, brogues, casual suede slip-on shoes and, at first, two-tone leather shoes, and sandals.

Most sports clothes did not alter very much from those of previous periods. Hunting clothes were similar to those worn in the late 1920s and consisted of riding jackets or single-breasted frock coats, or double-breasted morning coats with breeches or jodhpurs and riding boots. Stiff bowler hats were worn to protect the head.

For shooting, tweed jackets were popular worn with breeches or plus-fours. Deerstalker hats or tweedy cloth caps completed the wardrobe.

For riding, hacking jackets which had full skirts but were made in lounge jacket styles were worn. They were longish and the skirts could have either a centre back seam and vents, or two side slits for easier movement. Jodhpurs became general, more so than riding breeches, and the riding caps were usually of velvet, but reinforced so that they were hard.

Cricket gear was still white flannel trousers and shirts with canvas or buckskin shoes. Sweaters and caps with the club colours were also worn, and blazers usually had the club badge embroidered on the top breast pocket.

Tennis outfits varied very little from cricket clothes, apart from the cap, but gradually flannel trousers were replaced by white shorts. Shirts were usually worn open necked and white V necked sweaters or pullovers could be worn over them.

Football outfits still consisted of wool or cotton shirts

Belted raincoat with set-in sleeves, tabbed at the wrists. A soft tweed hat, breeches, stockings and brogues complete this country outfit

with round necks and knee length shorts which became shorter in the late 1940s. High socks in the club colours were also worn.

For golfing, casual clothes sufficed, as trousers were generally worn instead of the older traditional plus-fours and windcheaters replaced the Norfolk jacket.

For the seaside flannel trousers and blazers were general. Light coloured linen suits, originating in the United States and known as 'Palm Beach' suits were also worn in the 1940s. Very often, especially towards the 1950s, shorts became more popular than trousers, and bush jackets, modelled on the lines of tropical military uniforms and made of a strong cotton or twill, could be worn without shirts beneath. They resembled shirts in having shirt type collars and could have short sleeves with cuffs. Polo or roll necked shirts were quite often worn with casual linen cotton trousers.

For bathing, the one piece costumes that had the sides so cut out as to form a Y shape at the back were gradually superseded by swimming trunks during the War.

Yachting became less popular, as the trend was towards small boats and dinghies, so trousers or shorts and shirts with woollen pullovers sufficed. Oilskins were worn in bad weather.

For skiing, protective clothing was essential, so the trousers were made of a waterproof material and styled to fit neatly into the boot tops. Jackets, also in a proofed material, were tight at the wrists and zipped up the front to the neck. Anoraks were beginning to be worn. Thick socks were made of natural oiled wool which was water repellent.

As motoring became more general and was no longer regarded as a sport, special motoring clothes were no longer worn. With the spread of motoring, hats, umbrellas and sticks decreased in use, and shorter coats were found to be more practical for driving.

Beach wear, c. 1939

FOOTWEAR

The clothing coupons, which also embraced footwear, curtailed to a great extent new styles of shoes. Brown or black laced leather shoes as well as brogues continued to be worn, although suede instead of leather became more acceptable. Most shoes or boots had rounded toes, although they did tend to become slightly pointed.

From about 1947 new styles gradually appeared. Tall elastic-sided boots covering the ankles were popular. The elastic gussets at the sides allowed for easier putting on of the

Casual style jacket with contrasting coloured trousers, c. 1950

Crew cut hairstyle, c. 1950

Film stars set the male hairstyle trends in the 1940s

boots as they had no fastenings at all. Thick crepe soled shoes were also worn and some had strap and buckle fastenings.

Rubber galoshes which had been worn over shoes in rainy weather became less popular, although high rubber Wellington boots remained in vogue, especially for country wear.

In the summer, for leisure wear, sandals were worn. These were at first just lightweight shoes with a pattern punched out, and instead of the heel or quarter (the back part of the shoe) filled in, it was open with just a strap to support the sandal. Later the fronts of the shoes or sandals were also left open with wide straps to hold the soles to the feet.

During the War years socks, instead of reaching to mid-calf, reached to just above the ankles, but after the War, some again became longer, but by then they were elasticated at the tops, thus lessening the need for suspenders. Socks were generally made of silk, wool, rayon or cotton, and later of nylon or nylon mixtures which made them longer lasting. Knee length woollen stockings were still worn with plus-fours. Many otherwise plain socks and stockings were decorated up the sides with clocks, or they could have fancy designs on the borders. Stripes were always popular.

HAIRSTYLES

Hair was usually cut short and brushed with a parting on the left side. By the 1940s wavy hair was very fashionable, and straight hair was coaxed into waves. Film stars set many of the new trends and these were copied by many. Although beards were unfashionable, straight handle-bar moustaches as worn by many RAF pilots and army officers remained popular amongst civilians for some years after the War.

The trend for longer hair began in the middle 1940s when hair was full on top and the sides, although the shorter crew-cut styles still prevailed. These were also known as GI cuts. This was hair cut short all over. As the hair was gradually allowed to grow slightly longer and somewhat tousled in appearance it became known as a Feather Crew or Ivy League style.

After the War the 'Teddy Boys' with their Edwardian style of dress wore their hair longer at the sides and brushed it back towards the centre.

HEADWEAR

Many men, especially amongst the younger generation, ceased wearing hats after the War.

23

Bowler hats, always basically the same shape, but with only subtle alterations in the crown and brim curving up at the sides, were mainly worn for smartness in the City and on formal occasions with dark lounge suits.

Top hats, mainly for race meetings and weddings, were almost always in grey or fawn cloth; the sides were slightly less concave than previously and were about 10 cm high.

Homburg hats with stiffer brims than previously and crowns with less pinched-in indentations were still worn. Black homburgs were often worn instead of the gibus with dinner clothes (the gibus was a collapsible opera hat). Trilby hats, popularized by Sir Anthony Eden, later Lord Avon, and known as Eden hats, were similar to homburgs and worn for the same types of occasion throughout the period. They were made softer than homburgs. The brims were generally edged in silk or braid.

Snap brim hats with either a narrow binding or more usually without any, were similar in design to trilbys, with the brim turned down in front and up at the back.

Pork pie hats which had a circular instead of a longitudinal dent in the crown, originated in the United States. They were a more informal type of hat.

Hats made of felt, which had been scarce during the War, again became popular after the War and were made in a variety of colours.

Cloth caps were still worn with small peaks in front, especially by schoolboys as part of their uniform, and they were also popular amongst cricketers.

ACCESSORIES
Gloves were no longer worn as fashion accessories but merely as useful and protective practical articles against the cold in winter. Many gloves were hand or machine knitted, or they could be made of a thickish leather and lined in a fleecy

Tweed country hat

Homburg

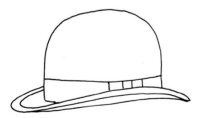

Felt Derby or bowler hat

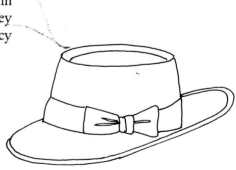

Pork pie felt hat

On the left is a typical war-time sight of a man in uniform. This soldier is a Royal Marine in embarkation kit. The lady on the right is wearing a heavy tweed overcoat with a belt, large patch pockets and high revers. Her hair is long, and curled under. The 1941-1942 period

The lady on the left is wearing a knee length two piece suit with the typical squared shoulders. The hat, gloves and scarf all matched. The shoulder handbag was made of plaited straw. The central figure is an officer of the R.A.F. in a greatcoat and a peaked service cap.

The lady on the right is in a Utility dress with a contrasting yoke and edging to the patch pockets. The sleeves are short and set in. It is in a shirtwaister style with the skirt fairly full. c.1943

Silk top hat

Topper for formal wear

material. Driving gloves, often of unlined leather could have the backs of string. Many gloves were fastened at the wrists with a button, although straps were also usual, and a gap was often seen on the back of the hand.

Scarves could be of wool or silk, the latter in white mainly for evening wear. The scarves could be plain or patterned, paisley designs being fashionable, and club colours were also very popular.

Spats made of drill or canvas, mainly in grey or white, were only worn occasionally at the beginning of the War for very formal weddings. They were a shoe covering, buttoned together on the outside edge, being held down under the foot with a strap and buckle.

Walking sticks as a fashionable addition ceased to be carried, but they were still carried by some elderly gentlemen. Umbrellas also were only carried when the weather so dictated. They were carried closely rolled and often had a matching tubular-like covering which fitted over the umbrella, the bottom being left open for the ferrule to pass through. Cane handles were popular, especially if the joints of the cane were prominent, or the curved handles could be covered in leather.

Handkerchiefs when worn as a fashion accessory were generally visible in a top breast pocket. They could have coloured borders and were made of either silk or linen. Fake handkerchiefs were also sometimes used in top pockets instead of real ones. These were made so that just the points showed above the pocket and were mounted on a stiff piece of paper which was insterted into the pocket.

Pocket watches were rarely seen except for occasional wear with dress suits. Wrist watches with metal or leather straps were generally worn; they could be either oblong, round or square in shape.

Tie-pins were occasionally worn with long ties to hold them in place. They were generally of gold with an ornamented head.

Cuff links were still used for shirt cuffs that did not fasten with buttons, or they could be worn with buttoned cuffs if there was a buttonhole present on each side.

With the increased popularity of motor cars, key rings became more ornate with leather fobs or charms attached.

Pocket cigarette cases became less fashionable as the cigarette packets in which cigarettes were bought became stronger. Pocket cigarette lighters began to supersede matchboxes.

The lady on the left is in a square cut jacket reaching the hips and fastened with three buttons; the shoulders are padded. Her trilby type felt hat is worn at an angle and her sling bag is of hide and fairly large. The man is wearing a siren suit and tin helmet for rescue work. The girl on the right is in overalls and a scarf ready for factory work. c. 1942-43

Women

Renovated dress made from various materials

Throughout the War years of 1939 to 1945, shortages of materials and the restrictions caused by clothing coupons controlled the style of clothing available. In fact coupons did not finally disappear until 1949. War work in the factories and Armed Forces also made practical women's clothing a necessity.

In 1941 utility clothes made their first appearance. These were made with the minimum of material, smaller hems and narrower seams, and were labelled with a double CC and 41 (CC41 – Clothing Control 1941). The materials used, however, were of a reasonable quality and individuality was not entirely omitted although the designs were plain and simple. As fashions were fairly restricted throughout the period, new styles could only be expressed in coupon-free accessories and make-up. Nevertheless many dresses were ingeniously renovated and remade so as to give them a new dimension. Also, new fashions were still being created by British and exiled French couturiers for export to the United States and the new designs could be seen on the cinema screens and in fashion journals in Great Britain.

British clothes styles were divided into two separate groups – high fashion, which was designed mainly for export, and the fashion that the ordinary woman in the street wore. The high fashion compared favourably with French fashion after the War, partially due to the fact that many French fashion designers had fled to England. High fashion garments not only set new trends, but also acted as advertisements for

British materials such as English woollens and Scottish tweeds. Mass production made a link between the two groups. It had become so organised that designers began to design specifically for the 'ready-to-wear' trade as well as for their more exclusive clientele.

From the end of the 1930s and the beginning of the 1940s styles became more severe with wider, padded shoulders to give a square look; French fashions were beginning to be less of an influence.

Longer upswept hairstyles became popular and there was a marked improvement in make-up. Darker face powders and matching nail varnish and lipstick became available.

In the late 1940s pleats became so popular that they appeared in skirts, blouses and jackets, and could be placed at all angles from horizontal to vertical and even diagonally.

After the War new man-made fibres made their appearance for clothing, the most notable being nylon. Also after the War fashions changed: the social climate altered and was reflected in the new fashions, especially in 1947 when Dior's 'New Look' captivated the world.

Femininity was restored with wasp waists, full skirts and a soft shoulder line. As skirts became fuller, coats became more bulky, and hats smaller and neater looking. Strapless evening gowns replaced the square military cuts of the War years.

DAY DRESSES

Shift dresses which fell from the shoulders were gathered at the natural waistline with a belt or sash. Petticoat dresses were short enough to reveal their embroidered underskirts.

By the 1940s the length of skirts was about 40 cm from the ground. Very full skirts were not very popular at this time, most of them being straight or just slightly flared. Pleats, however, were popular. The skirts were close fitting to the hips with fitted waists which could have a waistband.

Day dresses were fairly plain in the 1940s. They could be tailored and were almost always worn with belts, either of matching fabric or leather. Pinafore dresses were worn over blouses, and shirt-waisters became quite general wear towards the end of the 1940s. These were made with a buttoned-down-the-front bodice with a collar, and joined to a skirt that continued the fastening with buttons down to the hem. Sheath dresses which had a straight line without being waisted, and were in one piece, were often sleeveless and had a square cut neckline. These styles came into fashion in the late 1940s and early 1950s.

Plain day dress with belt at waist c. 1940

The man on the left is in a double-breasted Chesterfield overcoat with the wide revers with buttonholes: there are welted pockets at each side as well as a breast pocket. The hat is a felt trilby with a hatband. The lady is in a summer dress with short puffed sleeves and a small Peter Pan type collar; the hat is a turban type. The newsvendor in the background is wearing a loose overcoat and a scarf round his neck. On his head is a cap with a small peak. c. 1939

The man is an RAF flying officer and the girl on the right an ATS officer. The lady in the centre is wearing an off-the-face halo hat and a dress with a tabbed shoulder yoke; the shoulders are padded and square. c. 1942

New Look flannel suit with basqued jacket and taffeta off-the-shoulder cocktail dress, c. 1948

For afternoon wear day dresses were more feminine in appearance, having a gentler outline. Afternoon dresses often had a corselet waist which was boned and fitted and was often raised above the natural waist level. Peplums were also usual. Although dress collars were not much worn just before the War, they again became fashionable in the 1940s. Bodices which were tight fitting in the early 1940s became more bloused a little later, this effect being achieved by tucking and shirring.

Due to the shortages of materials the skirts were of a scanty style. They were fairly straight with kick pleats behind or a few pleats in the front. Neither pleating nor flares were very full, and often shirring was used at the waist to give a fuller effect. Tucks at the waistline also helped to achieve this effect. Skirts were fairly short reaching just about 45 cm from the ground. By about 1942 real or sham pockets at hip level accentuated the hips and therefore gave the waist a smaller appearance.

Around 1944 frills and peplums were used in skirts to give a bustle effect at the back. By 1945 and the end of the War, skirts had become a little longer with a straighter silhouette, although fullness or drapery from the hips was fashionable. 1946 saw skirts just below knee level, small waisted and fairly tight fitting with hip pockets or gathering at the sides. Front inverted pleats or unpressed pleats were also worn. The waistlines were often with an attached belt which could come to a point in the front, or have a slight upward curve, similar to the Swiss belt.

In 1947 the 'New Look' was introduced by Christian Dior in Paris. It was remarkable because not only was it his first collection, but also, although there was still a shortage of materials, a great deal was required for the full, wide skirts. His style of clothing was a reaction to the austerity of the War years. It made fashions really feminine again. Shoulders, instead of being square, became sloped — more natural and rounded than the square military styles of wartime — whilst waists were made to look tiny with the emphasis on busts and hips. Necklines were low and plunging and some dresses had three-quarter length batswing sleeves. The skirts became longer, reaching the calves, about 27 cm from the ground, and very full with the hips being padded to give extra bouffant results, and so emphasise the waistline. A variation had a bustle effect at the back.

The lady on the left is wearing an off-the-shoulder plunging neckline calf-length dress of the New Look. Her hat is small crowned with a very wide brim, while her gloves are long and ruched from the wrists to the elbows, c. 1947. The lady on the right is wearing a mid-calf dress with a pleated skirt; the collarless bodice is loose fitting and the set-in, almost to the wrist sleeves, loose. She is carrying a large flat handbag.

Short-sleeved dress with a sloping shoulder line and mid-calf hemline, c. 1949

The Dior gowns were so stiffened and padded that they could stand up on their own. For example, accordion pleated skirts had an inner pleated ruffle in the waistband so that the pleats fanned out sharply from the waist, whilst others were fitted with a whalebone corselet. Jackets or tops were padded at the shoulders to give an oval shape whilst padding just above the waist helped achieve the hourglass silhouette.

Old dresses were hastily renovated with matching or contrasting bands of materials inserted or added to the hemline. Narrow skirts were adapted to give a hobble line with emphasis on the hips being given by panniers or side pockets. Dirndl style skirts were also very popular.

By 1949 skirts had become a little shorter, reaching about 32 cm from the ground. Hip padding was less used, being replaced by large pockets and drapery to give the required fullness. Tight skirts had apron type overskirts or loose hanging panels.

Skirts became even shorter by 1950 when they finally reached about 40 cm from the ground, but they were mainly straight with added pockets, peplums and overskirts which were slightly shorter. Many had a diagonal line, being cut on the cross, and draped overskirts were also popular. Skirts were often fastened at the side with a zip or press-studs hidden by a placket.

The bodices of day dresses were often yoked and could be shirred at the shoulders and at the neckline which could be in a variety of shapes: round, square or V shaped. Turned-down collars were popular and shirt type tops with collar and revers and a fastening down the front were also much in vogue. Belts or waistbands were usual. Day dresses often had matching jackets or boleros.

For afternoon wear tailored dresses with matching jackets were often made in lightweight men's suiting materials.

The shoulder line on dresses became more sloped, and in the 1941-1943 period collars were quite small and sometimes even absent. Horizontal shirring or gathering was fashionable at the bust in the same period, and between 1944 and 1945 bloused and full gathered effects were popular. Cross-over bodices were also in evidence with the front of the skirts sometimes having a pleated panel inserted.

Dresses were often made in two different materials and colours, being conversions from perhaps two dresses. For instance the sleeves and skirt could be in a contrasting colour to the rest, or the bodice and skirt be different to the sleeves.

Close-fitting dolman-sleeved dress with diagonal fastening to give the appearance of extra fullness, c. 1949-50

There were endless ways of altering and converting clothes. 'Make do and mend' had become the slogan.

Cowl necklines were also popular. By 1946, after the War, the bustline had become more defined and shoulders, instead of being so square, became rounder and more sloped in line.

Basques and peplums were often cut in one with the bodices, and tucks or pleats from the bustline to the hips were also popular. Still fashionable were the one-sided drapes. The whole impression was of a longer and softer silhouette.

ENSEMBLES

Matching coats and jackets were very fashionable, as also were boleros. These were quite often of materials to match the dresses. These coatees were generally loose fitting and square cut; they hung straight from the shoulders and were generally left undone, although buttons and buttonholes were present. Fitted jackets, some with belts, were also fashionable. The length of these garments ranged from to the waist to about hip length, although boleros were shorter, either just above or to the waist. The fronts of boleros were often rounded although squared fronts were also worn. Boleros could be collarless or with collars and sometimes even with revers.

By the 1940s it became the fashion for dresses to be made to look like two-piece dresses, skirts and tops often being of differing colours and materials. Two piece dresses often comprised tunic dresses with blouses or skirts, and tunic blouses which were shorter than the skirts and were generally fastened at the back.

Skirts with matching high necked tops that could have small round collars were also popular. These high necked tops usually buttoned in the front and could be basqued and belted. Quite often there were two breast pockets present.

One piece dresses with matching jackets were very fashionable from the beginning of the 1940s. The jackets could be short bolero styles or the longer hip length variations. Jackets were also worn with skirts and trousers or slacks. In 1940 jackets became longer than previously and could be buttoned high up with wide lapels and small turned-down collars. They were often single-breasted with broad padded shoulders Bloused effects were fashionable and military styles became discernable as the War progressed. The style and cut of jackets became quite masculine.

Skirts were made of various materials, for instance, tweeds

Bolero type jacket with spotted blouse and a slim skirt with large pockets to accentuate the hips. A large hat over turban headwear and gauntlet gloves complete the ensemble, c. 1942

Utility costume, c. 1942

Three piece ensemble consisting of skirt, jacket and coat, early 1940s, and belted swagger coat with turned-back sleeve cuffs and patch pockets

for hardwearing country wear, whilst town suits were made in a lighter weight of material — men's suiting being ideal. Quite often these suits were also fur trimmed. If meant to be worn under a coat in winter, a popular material was the less bulky but equally fashionable wool jersey.

Jackets had long or three-quarter length, fairly tight sleeves which could be fashionably wrinkled below the elbows. Magyar and Raglan styles were also modish. Squared shoulders, which had begun to appear in the late 1930s, became popular in the 1940s with raised shoulders, reflecting the mood of determination which was thus symbolized.

Towards the end of 1940 Molyneux and Paquin, both French dress designers, made their first British collections. Captain Molyneux, an Irishman who opened his own fashion house in Paris after the First World War, designed a new style of jacket dress with the blouse and skirt attached. Paquin, who also designed lingerie, was one of the first designers to use fur as a trimming on suits and coats.

Slim-looking straight skirts with slight flares from the hips, or pleating, were worn. They had darts and seams from the waist to give a better fit, and reached about 40 cm from ground level. Skirts were also quite often straight with an inverted pleat in the front from hip level to give extra fullness and ease of movement. Skirts not part of a two piece suit were worn with jumpers or blouses over which could be worn jerkins or jackets. They reached approximately 40 cm from the ground and were made similarly to suit skirts, straight or slightly flared or pleated, and could have hip yokes. Pockets either side in the front were also popular, and if belts were worn they were often of the same material as the skirts themselves. Divided skirts gradually became more accepted apparel, especially as the War progressed.

Trousers for women also began to make their appearance, and were fastened at the side with a zip hidden by a placket.

Blouses could be worn loosely over skirts or could be tucked in. They were made in many different styles, like shirts buttoning down the front, for instance, or cross-over with a sash. Sleeves could be long with wristbands or cuffs that were buttoned, or they could be short and puffed.

Collars were sometimes quite plain with pointed or rounded fronts. Cowl collars were worn with blouses that had back fastenings.

Knitwear became very popular, being both hand and machine made. All kinds of garments were made in knitted

The lady on the left is in an ensemble with a straight skirt and draped overbodice, the drapery towards the back and one side. A large fur is around the shoulders and the muff is matching. The lady on the right is wearing a beret and a slim straight skirt. The blouse has a frilled front and cuffs.

materials: cardigans, suits with matching coats that had collars, lapels and even pockets, jumpers and matching cardigans, either plain or with designs and belted. Jumpers and matching cardigans were known as twin sets. Dungarees and siren suits could both be made of knitted stockingette material. Skirts could also be made in stockingette.

The bodice parts of jacket dresses were generally basqued and with either pockets or drapery. Turned-down collars as well as collarless bodices were worn. Amongst the more popular fashions were V or rounded necklines as well as cowled or heart shaped ones. By about 1948 square necked bodices sometimes had a diagonal front, fastening at the waist. By 1950 horseshoe shaped necklines were fashionable, and yoked bodices were also worn. Low necklines were often filled in with modesty vests or 'dickies'.

Dress sleeves were fairly plain, almost any length, and usually fairly tight fitting. They were raised with padding at the shoulders. Bishop sleeves gathered on to a wristband were also fashionable in the early 1940s. From about 1946 fuller sleeves became more popular and in 1947 puffed and padded sleeves became less modish as a softer look came in. Although sleeve cuffs were not so popular at first, by about 1949 they were again in vogue. Kimono, Magyar and dolman type sleeves were seen quite frequently in the early 1950s.

Coat dresses that opened down the entire front were made of a variety of heavy materials such as suiting, corduroy, heavy wools and jerseys. They were generally closed with buttoning down to the hem and were made in various styles. Shirt-waist designs were popular. Pockets at the hips, either patch or inserted in the pleats, as well as waist belts were in evidence.

Jacques Fath, in 1948, created another style, a hobble skirt, which had been fashionable previously. This was most impractical in the modern age, but the pencil skirt was successfully introduced as a fashion and variations on it remained in vogue throughout the 1950s.

SUITS AND COSTUMES

In the early 1940s suit jackets usually reached the hips and were fastened with between three and seven buttons. The fronts were generally square cut, but could be slightly rounded. Patch pockets were popular; slanting pockets with flaps were also quite usual. Jackets could be belted, or sometimes the belt was set in. A military effect during the War was accomplished by the use of squared shoulders, belts, patch pockets

Dress with bishop sleeves and a pillbox hat. Late 1940s

and by the general severity of styles as well as the small collars and lapels. Utility styles were quite plain and simple, single-breasted, and fastening with no more than three buttons which could come quite high.

In 1943 the jackets became a little shorter, ending just above the hips, and lapels became wider. Some jackets became so short that they resembled boleros, and could even have three-quarter length sleeves. The shorter jackets could also have waistcoat style fronts.

In 1947 when the New Look was so popular, the jackets became slightly longer again with padding at the hips, large pockets and waists more accentuated. Padding at the shoulders became less prominent as rounded and softer shaping appeared. The front edges of the jacket at the hem were also more often to be seen with rounded corners. Alternatively flared basques were often added to the jackets at the waist. Jackets when closed high at the neck often only had small collars that could be rounded.

Two piece suit with belted and bloused jacket, with blouse collar and cuffs turned over the jacket, c. 1948

By about 1950 classical style jackets were popular. These had stepped collars and revers and could be either single- or double-breasted. They usually had slit pockets with flaps and were fitted at the waist. Straight or box type jackets were also worn as well as bloused jackets with belts.

Necklines became more adventurous with horseshoe shapes and fill-ins, or sailor type collars. If the décolletage was fairly low, 'dickies' were often inserted. Kimono or dolman type sleeves as well as three-quarter length styles were all worn.

Suit or costume skirts were fairly plain and about 45 cm from the ground. They became slightly longer until in 1946 they were approximately 30 cm. For town wear skirts were slightly shorter than for the country. At the beginning of the era skirts were straight with kick pleats to give freer movement, or the slim effect was kept with knife pleating all round and inverted pleats both back and front. When the New Look came into fashion in 1947, and skirts became longer, they also became fuller, with gores and pleats or cut in a circular fashion. Pleats, bustles and flares were much in vogue. Wrap-over styles were also worn and by 1949 skirts again became slimmer with overskirts at the back, and pleating at the sides only. Some straight skirts had just a small slit at the back.

Top coats or overcoats were very often made of the same materials as the two piece costumes, a popular material being men's suiting which was more readily available throughout the War years, due to the fact that most men were in uniform.

Classical style costume in the New Look, c. 1950

Cardigan suits also became popular, often made of jersey or knitted by hand. The skirts were usually fairly straight and plain, whilst the jackets buttoned high to the neck which could be collarless.

JUMPERS AND KNITWEAR

During the War, especially during air raids, knitting and crocheting by hand became really popular pastimes, as it not only kept people's minds off the War, but also saved clothing coupons. Old knitted garments could be unravelled and knitted up into new ones, sometimes with extra wool added, making the sleeves in a contrasting colour perhaps, or knitting in designs.

Twin sets comprising a plain short-sleeved jumper, usually with a round collar, and a matching long-sleeved cardigan which usually buttoned high to the neck, were extremely popular.

Jumpers were not only made of wool, but could be of silk or cotton. They could be hand or machine knitted or crocheted in open lacework designs as well as in various patterns and colours. Necklines could be high with roll collars, or cowls, V necks, polo or crew necks. Shoulders, during the War years, were very often padded. Sleeves were either set in or of the Raglan type.

Cardigans and jumpers were made to match in both colour and design; cardigans could also be worn over dresses or blouses. They might be buttoned high to the neck with a plain round neckline or have a small Peter Pan type collar. A V opening was also fashionable, either with or without a collar. Revers were also sometimes seen. Lumber jackets or windcheaters were generally of a thicker wool and had high necks buttoning down the front or on one side from the shoulder to an attached waistband. 'Sloppy Joe' was a name given to a type of loose knitted cardigan — more of a short coated style in fact.

Boleros, dresses, suits and skirts could all be of knitted materials. From about 1945 Fair Isle patterns, which had been popular in the 1920s but lost favour in the 1930s, again became fashionable for all knitwear.

From the end of the 1940s cardigans and jumpers became longer. Evening blouses, usually of a silky openwork design, often had low square décolletages. Knitted dresses and skirts could even be pleated, or the knitted design so made as to simulate pleating.

Classical twin set and turban head-dress of the 1940s

SKIRTS

Skirts were very popular and were worn with either blouses or jumpers. They even became more general than dresses, being more practical, especially during the time of shortages of materials. Changes in wardrobe could be more easily achieved: one skirt could be worn with several different tops and vice versa, thus relieving the monotony.

Skirts in general were similar in style to the skirts which were a part of suits and costumes, and also about 45 cm off the ground, until 1947 when they became longer to reach only about 28-30 cm. By the end of the 1940s skirts again became straighter and shorter to about 40 cm above the ground. Dirndl skirts (often made of curtain materials) were very popular either with or without pockets. They could be cut straight and gathered on to a waistband, or cut on the cross to give a greater fullness without the bulk at the waistline. In the mid 1940s the waistbands were often curved or pointed in the front, like Swiss belts.

TROUSERS

Women discovered how practical trousers were, especially during the Blitz period. They were worn for work as well as at night when they were extremely practical, useful and warm in air-raid shelters. They were made with or without turn-ups, but seldom worn with high heeled shoes. They were generally fairly wide and loose fitting until 1949 when tapered and narrow trousers became fashionable. Slacks, if worn for more elegant occasions, were sometimes made of old long evening skirts.

Trouser suits with jackets, similar to suit jackets, or with flared overtunics became the mode. They were worn as 'separates', that is with blouses, jumpers, jackets. Skirts were also sometimes made to match the trousers and could be worn as an alternative.

Blue jeans, first so popular in the United States, made their first appearance in England about 1947, and were worn only by young girls as holiday wear.

Knee length divided skirts were an alternative to slacks and more practical than skirts for sports and general activities. Shorts, worn in the summer, reached to mid-thigh.

BLOUSES

As the War years progressed, so blouses and skirts or jackets became increasingly popular and practical. In the mid 1940s

Trousers and blouse worn first in the War years

white blouses worn with black skirts were especially popular, although generally all colours were worn.

Blouse sleeves were very often puffed at the shoulders and could be long or short. Long full sleeves often ended with either cuffs or wristbands. The cuffs could be buttoned and folded over, edged with lace or frilling, or just plain with pointed or rounded corners. Raglan, bishop or kimono sleeves as well as sleeveless blouses were all seen. Necklines varied greatly from high and rounded with a variety of different colours to cowl necked or boat shaped. Cross-over blouses were also fashionable.

Blouses could be long and worn over skirts or trousers in Russian style with a belt, or basqued and worn either over or tucked into the skirts. They could even be pouched over the top of a skirt. Blouses were also made in a waistcoat style without sleeves, or made like shirts.

Afternoon and evening blouses were made in more elaborate ways, with frilled collars and cuffs if the sleeves were long. Jabots, tucks or fine pleating down the front, either horizontal, vertical or diagonal, as well as yokes were very popular.

Evening coat, c. 1939

EVENING AND FORMAL WEAR
From 1939 into the early 1940s, evening skirts worn with elaborate tops and jackets or boleros were more popular than evening dresses made in one, although some short evening dresses were to be seen with full skirts. These were sometimes long dresses cut short. On the whole evening dresses became much more informal, and by 1943 long dresses were seldom seen.

On formal occasions evening dresses were long and reached the ground. Many dresses had back closures from the bodice down. Low décolletages or bodices with just shoulder-straps could be covered with short matching boleros. Heart shaped fronts were often lace edged. Sequins were a very popular decoration and were added in various motifs on the bodice and also often on the skirt, either in panels down the front or around the hemline.

Cap sleeves as well as short puffed or long sleeves were as popular as decorated shoulder-straps. The waists of evening dresses could come up to a point in the front where the skirt and bodice met, and either side of the point was gathered to give more fullness. Large bows were also a great favourite as decoration. Shirring or gathering in the front, even without the raised waist, was very popular for bodices.

Skirts could be straight or gored, having drapery over the hips. Low décolletages were fashionable, and sometimes the backs were quite bare, the opening reaching to just above the waist.

About 1945 heart shaped décolletages were fashionable as well as cowl necklines, and off-the-shoulder styles became the mode. Boned strapless tops or halter necks were also in vogue.

Tulip skirts were worn which consisted of a plain skirt with overlapping curved panels. Long straight skirts sometimes had a slit up one side to facilitate dancing at supper dances. By 1947 uneven hemlines began to appear with the fronts often slightly shorter than the backs. Bustles and hip drapery were also popular.

By about 1948 shorter dance frocks were in vogue, reaching the ankle or just above (ballet length). Tight fitting bodices could have very low décolletages and wide low collars, or they could be strapless and boned. Fichu effects were also much worn.

For balls very wide and full skirts with diaphanous overskirts and bodices were usual. The bodice and skirt could be embroidered with sequins or sparkling artificial stones. By 1950 strapless or draped bodices were very fashionable, and the bouffant skirts could just reach mid-calf. Halter necklines or just one shoulder left bare were also popular.

For dinner wear dresses could be long or three quarter length. Certain dresses could be worn in the daytime and in the evening an added skirt or overskirt which was generally flared was often worn over a straighter shorter dress, the overskirt being longer in order to convert the dress into evening wear. Long skirts were also popular with evening blouses which could have bishop sleeves. These blouses were often made of a soft flimsy material and could be decorated with sequins. Lace knitted jumpers were often made up with metal thread in the materials used. Dinner dresses could have matching boleros or basqued jackets of a contrasting colour.

Coat dresses for dinner wear were also worn with wide necklines and large collars, buttoning down the entire front, including the full skirts. Long skirts and basqued bodices made separately were also seen. Some dinner dresses had skirts cut fairly straight and only reaching the calf.

Wedding dresses, until the beginning of the War, and for a little while longer, were long with large veils and orange blossom wreaths for the headwear. The gowns were usually of white satin or silk and lace and the sleeves long and tight

Ball dress, c. 1950

Ballet length dance frock, c. 1948

so always carry
your gas mask

ISSUED BY THE MINISTRY OF HOME SECURITY.

The lady on the left is in a two piece suit, the jacket reaching the hips and belted. The shoulders were becoming more square. Hair was worn fairly long with the front and sides up in curls. The gentleman is in a single-breasted lounge suit with just three buttons. No waistcoat was worn but the trousers still had turn-ups. The little girl is in a Brownie uniform of the period and is wearing knee-length socks and laced shoes. The whole family are carrying gas masks in boxes worn over their shoulders: gas masks and cases or containers became part of every wartime fashion, c. 1939

fitting. As the War progressed and more and more women joined the Armed Forces, uniforms or ordinary day dresses or suits were worn. The traditional white wedding dresses, if worn, were often borrowed. After the War, when the usual wedding dress was trained, with long or short sleeves and in various styles, the skirts could be either full or tight fitting. The headdress could be of orange blossom or feathers, or in a tiara style, and veils could either be long or just reach shoulder level.

Mourning dress, as such, had almost disappeared by the beginning of the 1940s except among older women who still wore black for a while. However at funerals it was general to wear a black suit or outfit, although light coloured stockings were permitted.

INFORMAL WEAR

Teagowns in the 1940s were, if worn, generally long sleeved with long skirts. However this fashion declined as the pace of life generally speeded up. Housecoats however were popular, made of a warm material, and these gradually replaced the teagown for informal evening wear. At first housegowns were worn for comfort after a day's work, and were ground length with a zip or button fastening, either to the waist and stepped into, or down to the hem. They were made in various styles, from the Princess style to loose versions. They could have belts or sashes and pockets were a useful addition. Sleeves could be of any length and anything from straight and tight fitting to bishop style.

By about 1949 the housecoats, or housegowns as they were known, had become more sophisticated and were made in more elaborate materials such as brocades. They could then also be in tent-like styles with full sleeves, and the skirts just reach the ankles. They became so elegant that they could also be worn as evening coats.

Cocktail dresses, worn in the early evening, were not much in evidence during the War years, but by about 1949 cocktail or short calf-length dinner dresses made of taffeta or silk were worn. The décolletage was low and often V shaped with a wide collar that covered the sleeveless shoulders. Bodices were generally fairly plain and the skirts full. Belts were also popular. If the skirts were not very full side drapery, usually on the left, was fashionable. Straight skirts often had loose panels, one at the front and one at the back.

Maternity dresses were fairly simple, with smocking at the

Housecoat with zip of the 1940s

bosom and then flared straight down. Many maternity skirts had a loose front panel to cover an open gap over the abdomen, and this was fastened with tapes or ties, according to the size required. Other styles were pleated with an adjustable underskirt, or they might have shoulder straps and be designed to hang loosely beneath smocks or loose blouses. Smock-like jackets were also popular.

CLOTHES DURING THE SECOND WORLD WAR

Air raid wardens were all issued with steel helmets painted dark green with the initials ARP (Air Raid Precautions), and ordinary civilians were encouraged to wear fibre helmets during air raids. The standard colours were khaki or black, but they could be painted in other colours.

Gas masks were issued to everyone and were issued in cardboard boxes with a string so that they could be carried over the shoulder. However most people resorted either to making or buying more robust containers made of American cloth or imitation leather with leather shoulder straps.

Winston Churchill, the wartime Prime Minister, popularized the wearing of siren suits. These consisted of trousers, jackets, and often hoods either attached or detachable, all made in one. These garments were fastened down the front. The long sleeves and the baggy trouser bottoms were gathered on to an elasticated band to give a snug fit. A belt was worn around the waist and patch pockets were invariably present. These siren suits were an extremely useful item of attire worn at nights during air raids in air raid shelters as they could be slipped on over nightwear or underclothes.

Dungarees or trousers were worn in the factory and for work on the land as well as in the public services, for instance by bus conductresses and the Armed Services. Smocks or long buttoned-through overalls were also worn by women who worked in canteens and similar places. Trousers gradually became accepted wear for uniforms and ordinary day wear in general.

Snoods and turban-like headscarves were highly recommended for wear over long hair, especially in factories where hair could get caught in the machinery.

Women had extremely ingenious ways of altering and renovating clothes to make them more fashionable in the War years. Old dresses had contrasting fronts inserted, or two dresses could be converted into one, with the bodice of one dress added to the skirt of another. Long sleeves could be

Army nurse and Women's Land Army uniforms, 1939-45

shortened. Evening dresses were shortened and the low décolletages altered to turn them into pinafore frocks to be worn with either jumpers or blouses beneath. Old greatcoats were reassembled into skirts and matching boleros, or shortened into jackets. When the New Look came in 1947 coats and dresses were lengthened with contrasting materials and panels inserted to give extra fullness.

Patchwork was also very popular for skirts and blouses, both in fabric and using knitted squares that could use up leftover scraps of wools and be made into all kinds of garments. Even coarse dishcloths and curtain materials (both free of coupons) were utilized in the making of garments.

SPORTS WEAR

As clothing had generally become more informal, mainly because of the Second World War, it was mainly the sports and leisure clothes that differed from ordinary day dress. However, sports wear did not alter very much in the period: the traditional styles mainly remained as there was less opportunity for sports.

From about 1939, just prior to the War, tennis skirts became shorter and were either flared or had sunray pleating

Golf outfit consisting of a pleated skirt and sleeveless jacket over a short-sleeved blouse, c. 1941

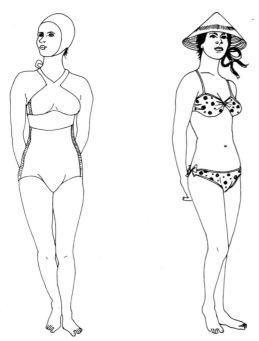

Knitted wool swimsuit and rubber bathing cap, c. 1941, and bikini worn with coolie type hat, c. 1948

Ballerina suit beach dress, c. 1940

and were worn over tight matching pants. These skirts became more popular than tennis shorts, although shorts could be worn beneath skirts that were buttoned down the front. Short dresses were also fashionable. Tennis outfits were always white, including the woollen pullovers that could be worn with either skirts or shorts.

For swimming silk lastex was used both for one piece suits and for bra and pants. This was an elasticated woven material. The two piece bra and pants costumes often had a flared skirt over the pants. Many one piece swimming costumes were backless or even strapless with the brassiere supported by whale bones. From about 1947 bikinis became popular. These were two piece costumes, but much briefer and more revealing than previous two piece costumes: both bra top and pants were very scanty, covering just the bare essentials.

For wear on the beach, blouses and slacks were popular, and playsuits consisting of one piece, the top and shorts in one. Skirts could be worn over these garments to make them look like summer frocks. Sun tops were fashionable from about 1948, these having a low brassiere-shaped décolletage and removable straps for sun bathing. These tops might form part of a dress or be separate and worn with skirts or slacks or shorts. Often matching jackets or boleros were also worn. Another style of sleeveless sun dress had, instead of the brassiere-shaped décolletage, a straight top with a frill and detachable shoulder-straps. Halter straps were also much in evidence.

For cycling, divided skirts were worn as well as shorts.

Golf clothing consisted mainly of skirts and jumpers. The skirts were fairly full with pleating, often only from the hips, the pleats above being stitched down to give a more shaped and smooth lined skirt. The material used was often a shower-proof poplin or tweed, and often matched the windcheaters which could be made reversible, so that a contrasting colour could also be seen. These jackets had elasticated waistbands and wrist cuffs, and zipped down the front. Collars were generally not large and turned down. Jersey jackets could be slightly longer and have a belt around the waist. By about 1949 tweed was also used for dresses. These often had a yoke at the shoulder and inverted pleats at the back of the bodice.

Riding jackets were fitted to the waist and had patch pockets; they were mannish in appearance and had small turned-down collars and revers. Often they were made of tweed. In the early 1940s close-cut narrow breeches were

Tennis shirt and shorts in one, c. 1941

The tennis outfit on the left consists of a white blouse and a short
white pleated skirt, c. 1948. The ski outfit in the centre is a round-
necked pullover worn beneath a waterproof jacket gathered at the waist
with elastic. The waterproof trousers are tucked into ski boots, c. 1949.
The girl on the right is wearing a cotton beach skirt over a matching
bikini, c. 1948

The New Look. On the left is the mid-calf length skirt and the jacket, ending at hip level, has soft rounded shoulders and a fitted waist. On the right is a coat in the New Look style with high stand-fall collar, deep cuffed sleeves. The coat is fitted to the waist and then flared out with flapped pockets to accentuate the hip line. c.1948

Off-the-peg clothes in the New
Look style. The outfit on the left is
a two piece costume with high
neckline and small turn-down
collar and large buttons down the
front of the jacket which is flared
from the close fitting waist. The
small hat worn towards the back of
the head is of simulated fur. The
stockings are fully fashioned and
the shoes court type.

The lady on the right is wearing a
fine organdy blouse with a pencil
skirt, calf length and high at the
front. The gloves and beret type
hat matched the skirt material.
c.1949-1950

worn, but by about 1947 jodhpurs which were loose fitting to the knee, forming 'wings' at the sides, and then tight to the ankles were worn. High necked pullovers and tweed jackets usually completed the outfit.

For winter leisure wear shirts were often worn under striped jumpers with the shirt collars over the rounded necks. Woollen gloves, scarves and caps knitted to match the jumpers were also popular. Loose, baggy trousers were tucked into thick woollen socks and wedge heeled shoes were fashionable towards the end of the 1940s.

UNDERWEAR

Underwear consisted of brassiere, briefs and suspender belts which were worn beneath the briefs. Vests were worn mainly in the winter for warmth. Petticoats and slips were worn as foundation garments so that unlined dresses and skirts would hang better.

Petticoats were full length with the tops shaped to the bosom. Sometimes the tops and the hems of the petticoats were of a lacy material. Slips from the waist were very full when worn with the New Look fuller dresses and skirts. Often more than one slip was worn to give extra fullness.

Tight waisted corselette, c. 1947

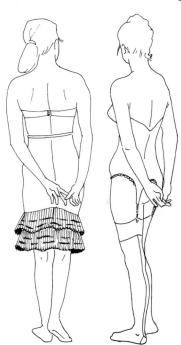

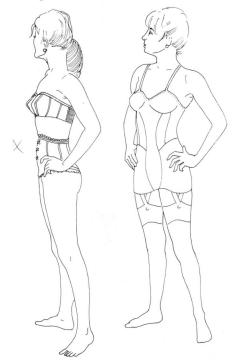

Chemise slip with pleated frills, c. 1949

Half slip with deep net pleated frill, c. 1949 and corselette, c. 1950

Strapless boned uplift brassiere and waist cincher or corselette with front lacing, c. 1947, and all-in-one brassiere and corset in lastex material, c. 1940

49

Brassieres could be made without straps and be boned, thus being self-supporting. Suspender belts were more popular than the restricting corsets with attached suspenders previously worn, and were made of a wide piece of material, either entirely or partially elasticated, with long and adjustable suspenders to hold up the stockings.

Nylon, which made such an impact on underwear, was originally discovered by accident in 1929 by a chemist, Dr W.H. Carothers who was trying to make a synthetic rubber for DuPont. It first came on the market in 1940 in the form of nylon stockings, and the word nylon became synonymous with stockings. Their advantage over silk stockings was that nylon was less shiny, cheaper to manufacture, and longer lasting, as well as easier to wash.

Lingerie was often made of nylon from the 1940s onwards, artificial fibres becoming even more popular than natural ones, although a mixture was often used. The advantage of man-made materials was that they were good insulators against both hot and cold weather, and were also drip-dry and needed little or no ironing.

Underslip

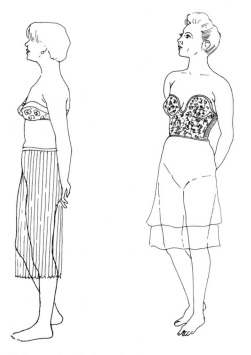

Half slip made of pleated nylon worn with a strapless brassiere, c. 1950, and boned brassiere with plunging neckline and uplift, c. 1945

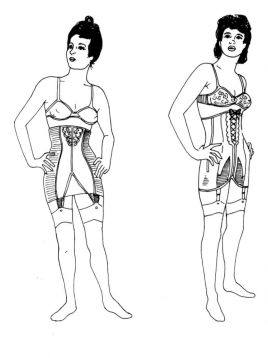

Tight-waisted suspender girdle, c. 1948, and corset with side zips and front lacing, c. 1939

Square-shouldered swagger coat, c. 1946

Overcoats began to have a military appearance with shoulder epaulettes, wide revers and patch pockets, some with flaps. The shoulder line was squarish and could be built up with padding. Coats with fitted waists and flared or pleated skirts sewn to a waistband were also popular. Swagger coats, fairly straight in the front, were full at the back. This effect was accomplished with pleats, or by cutting the material on the cross. Vertical slit pockets at the sides were usual.

As the War progressed coats remained austere, still with high shoulders and a military look. Revers could be short and pockets at an angle. Single- and double-breasted styles were both seen. Belts with buckles could be worn with the shaped coats. The looser types of coat could be of the wrap-over style with belts that tied in the front. Tie belts were as popular as belts that fastened with buckles and were used throughout the decade on coats that were fitted to the waist. The coat skirts could be made full by being cut on the cross or have pleats. If cut in one with the bodice, darts were inserted from hip to bust to give the coats a more tailored shape. Back pleats were also popular.

Some coats had detachable or attached hoods, and turned-back cuffs on the long sleeves. Capes were also sometimes worn.

Both double- and single-breasted coats in the early 1940s had squared shoulders, largish collars and revers. Pockets could be of the patch variety as well as the slit type, which could be set at an angle and have flaps. Dolman sleeves were seen as much as the set-in type. Swagger coats could be full or three quarter length. Short box-shaped coats were also popular.

French coat styles were very fashionable during the War years, designed by the French designers who had left their own country. For extra warmth many cloth coats had quilted linings.

Just before the end of the War, about 1944, coats became slightly shorter, knee length, and much fuller, with a belt around the waist. The collars also became larger. The square shoulders became softer in appearance and sleeves more close fitting. At the front, many coats just met edge to edge with no overlap. Yoked shoulders were also popular.

The swing of coats was more to the rear and waisted flared coats also followed these lines. From 1946 the sleeves became much wider and the armholes larger; dolman and bishop

Swagger coat with a flared back, c. 1947

sleeves came into fashion. Fur collars once more became the mode after the War when fur again became easier to obtain.

After 1947 three quarter length or slightly longer, but not full length swagger or full backed and waisted coats with belts were very popular. The tops of the coats were generally well fitted and large collars either with long points or in a shawl style were popular as were large pockets.

Tent style coats with the main fullness at the back, achieved either by pleating or by the cut became popular. They were mainly allowed to hang loosely or they could be belted. Sometimes there was a slit in the side seams for the belt to pass through, so that the belt passed either under the coat at the back and just pulled in at the front, allowing the back to flare, or else the reverse, with the belt showing at the back and fastened underneath the coat in the front, thus permitting the front to hang loosely. Many of these coats were made of two materials, thus also making them reversible.

Fur, either real or artificial, was widely used as a trimming on collars, cuffs and sometimes the edges of pockets. Fur or fur fabric lining was also in use. Fur jackets as well as three-quarter length fur coats with squared shoulders were worn. Some were belted. By 1946 collars on fur coats were less seen, although some roll collars were acceptable, but long revers were popular. Bishop sleeves and full backs were popular for fur coats. The silk or satin lining in the sleeves of fur coats was often gathered at the wrists to prevent the arms from getting cold if the coat sleeves themselves were full to the wrist. Fur capes were also worn.

Raincoats were mainly of the trench coat style, being double- or single-breasted and worn with buckled belts. Capes with hoods and the pockets placed inside were also practical. After the War, from about 1946, nylon became used much more for rainwear, as it was showerproof as well as light.

FOOTWEAR

Silk stockings ceased to be manufactured after 1941 when rayon, cotton and wool stockings were substituted. At first both cotton and rayon stockings were make to look like silk, but later they were produced in more fancy weaves and designs. At about the same time knee length and ankle socks were much worn, especially when the weather was not too cold, although in summer time neither socks nor stockings were worn a great deal. Leg make-up was used in the absence of stockings and a seam was even carefully painted down the

New Look coat flared from the waist, c. 1949

Multi-strapped shoe, c. 1948

Platform sandal with ankle fastening, c. 1948

centre back of the legs to aid the illusion of wearing stockings. Nylon stockings were first made in Great Britain in 1947 and silk stockings were again manufactured from 1948, but never really regained popularity being more expensive and less hardwearing than nylons.

Many shoes, until the War, had been imported from the United States and were made in a wide range of fittings. Heels were fairly low and wedges became very popular. A sensible and sturdy type of shoe increased in popularity, although sling back and peep-toe shoes were also worn. Most shoes had rounded or squared toes and were tied with shoe laces. Oxford, brogue and ghillie types were fashionable, as were also moccasins, a softer and less hardwearing type. Crepe soles as well as the higher platform variety were also in use.

Shoes could be made of suede as well as leather, and instead of being tied, have elastic inserted at the sides.

Ankle boots, often zip fastened in the front, and fleece lined, or with the inside of sheepskin and the outers of suede, were often worn by the wealthier classes in winter sports areas. These boots became popular during the War years as an effective protective covering for feet and ankles as they could easily be put on and were suitable both for bad weather and for air raid emergencies, especially during the cold winter nights.

Sandal type espadrilles, c. 1948

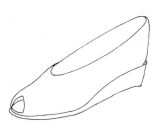

Open sandal with wedge heel, asymmetrical design and ankle straps, c. 1949

Court shoe with peep toes and wedge heel

Peep toed shoe with small platform and high heels

Round heeled Dutch type clog shoe, 1939-40

High fronted shoe with concealed elastic gore

Court shoe

For going-out and dressy occasions, high heeled court shoes were usual. They could be quite plain and sling-back. This meant that they were open at the back, with a heel strap that either fastened with a buckle at the side or was elasticated. Ankle straps also became fashionable. Ankle strap shoes were also backless with just a loop at the back to support the strap that went around the ankle and fastened in front.

Just after the War peep-toe styles appeared. The very front of the shoes had the toe piece cut away either in a curve or straight across to reveal the toes. Smart walking shoes could be high in the front with a tab concealing elastic which helped give the shoes a better fit. A large decorative bow in either leather or fabric was also sometimes attached to the shoe.

Sandals were made of leather or suede remnants, or of raffia or some other material, and the soles and heels could be of cork. Wedges and platform soles were popular. A popular style of sandal was with the front uppers in two wide strips of leather or fabric crossed over with a decoration at the centre and with ankle straps that crossed at the back.

As there was a shortage of leather, other materials such as strong fabrics and gaberdine, were used for shoe uppers, whilst soles and heels were often made of crepe rubber. Heels in the 1940s were generally fairly thick and straight. Just before the end of the War, about 1944, wooden soled shoes

Court shoe with asymmetrical design c. 1949

High heeled and platform sandal with ankle strap fastening

High backed lace-up shoe, c. 1941

Side-laced suede shoe with crepe sole, c. 1943

Evening shoe, c. 1940

Suede and leather court shoe, c. 1946

Two tone boot with high heel, c. 1948

Leather boot with side zip fastening, the top fur trimmed, c. 1949

Backless linen shoe, c. 1948

High tiered wedge sandal

were fashionable. These were often made similar to clogs. The wooden soles and heels were generally faced with rubber to give longer wear. 'Bouncers', a type of sports shoe, still popular, were made with the wedges built in. With high wedges being popular, it was fashionable to have a hole through the heel part, which was known as a 'loop' or 'flying buttress'.

The main characteristic of post-war footwear was that the shoes became narrower, with the heels higher and less clumsy. The fronts of the shoe uppers also reached higher. Often shoes, mainly court types, had very high and slender heels, with the fronts so low that the toes were almost visible. Asymmetric patterns in the front were also fashionable. The backs of shoes could also be semi-open in a lattice-like pattern.

From about 1947 shoe designers again became fashion conscious, especially the Italian designer Ferragamo, and the quality, which had been controlled, improved immensely. Higher heels and narrow toe shapes became the mode, although wedges, platforms and all the other open types of shoes with ankle or sling-back straps, remained popular. Walking shoes remained low heeled and serviceable.

The first plastic shoes made their appearance around 1949, and it was fashionable for sandals or evening shoes to have uppers in a clear plastic or vinyl.

Evening shoe, c. 1941

Shoe with a high wedge and a hole through the heel

Crepe wedge shoe, c. 1940

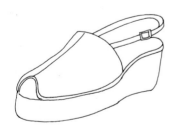

Casual shoe with a platform and a strap (sling-back) fastening, c. 1941

Fur lined and trimmed boot

High fur boot

HEADWEAR

The War years saw a real decline in the wearing of hats, and as no new styles appeared old hats sufficed for special occasions. When head covering was required, a scarf or square of material was usually worn. Scarves and kerchiefs were worn mainly for their practicability, especially to hold back the long hair of women working in factories.

Headscarves, which have retained their popularity to this day, were worn in many various ways. They were generally squares of either silk, cotton or a fine woollen material folded crossways with the long ends tied under the chin, or pulled around the head and tied under the hair with the short point of the scarf at the back. Another way of wearing headscarves was with the long ends brought to the front and tied on the top of the head catching the other corner under the bow or knot, the scarf actually being worn the reverse way, the long straight edge covering the head at the nape of the neck.

Snoods were also much worn, again generally for practical reasons. Snoods were a kind of hair net, but made of a thicker material, and worn towards the back of the head. They contained loose long hair or chignons. They could be worn for indoor as well as outdoor wear, and for dressy occasions were embellished with imitation stones or sequins as well as gold or silver thread. For outdoor wear they could also form part of a hat by being attached, not unlike the bavolet of previous times.

Shallow sailor hats, tied down, often with a narrow ribbon

Snood

Headsquare tied turban fashion, c. 1940

Broad striped halo hat, c. 1944

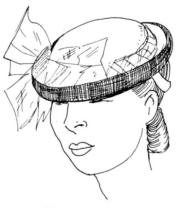

Small hat worn forward with a band at the back to secure it and net decoration, c. 1939

Turban, c. 1944

Kerchief worn peasant fashion,
c. 1941

American army fashion hat,
c. 1944

under the chin, and skull caps were both worn. Skull caps as well as soft hats were often either knitted or crocheted and might be worn with matching scarves and gloves.

Veils, either just covering the eyes or longer and tied under the chin, were often used as trimming on hats, as were ribbon loops, bows, artificial flowers and feathers. Fur trimming was also fashionable.

For the evening, little headwear was worn except for a few flowers, either real or artificial, and ribbons or tulle decorated with sequins. Flat pillbox hats with veils were worn in the late 1940s.

Hats in the early 1940s were mainly worn back off the face at an angle, but by about 1943 they were worn more forward. The crowns were sometimes quite high and pointed, whilst the brims could be large and floppy. Many hats were made of leather. Pillbox shaped hats and berets, some with small peaks, were all worn during the period. During the War years there was little trimming used, and although hats were not on coupons, the fashion for wearing them, except for special occasions, declined.

However, after the War, from about 1945, hat trimmings again became more elaborate, and the mode for wearing hats returned. Hat brims could be worn up or down. Toques, turbans and caps were all in vogue. Hats were often worn off the face and at a side slant; feather or plume trimmings on the side were very popular for quite a while.

In 1947, when the New Look made its first appearance,

Headwear, c. 1946

Skyscraper style hat, c. 1944

Pleated hat with ribbon trim,
c. 1944

hats were made in a great variety of styles. The sailor and Breton shapes always remained popular. Head hugging hats with off-the-face brims were made in cloche styles. Close fitting helmet or bonnet hats were also worn.

For summer wear small-crowned straw hats with enormous brims, like picture hats, were very fashionable. In winter the hats were smaller and could be pillbox shaped. By the late 1940s and early 1950s, hats were generally worn straight on the head with little or no tilt. Trilby or Robin Hood type hats were also worn in the 1940s.

Hat with attached scarf, c. 1947

Halo hat with a large bow, worn off the face, c. 1945

Flattish hat tilted forward, c. 1946

Tall beret-type veiled hat, 1940s

58

Small straw pillbox hat

Just after the War the hats were still flat and worn with a forward tilt, but about 1946 small hats were often worn towards the back, and in the winter could be draped with attached scarves. Sou'wester or fishergirl styles were worn towards the back of the head with the brims turned back.

With the development of civil air travel, air hostesses, who were noted for their smart appearance, wore hats and caps matching their suits, and these were usually designed by famous fashion houses.

Military type beret

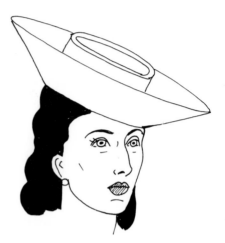

Beret worn at an angle

Sailor type hat, 1940s

Serrated straw hat, c. 1946

High built up toque-like hat, c. 1941

Off-the-face style hat, c. 1950

HAIRSTYLES

Hair was worn fairly short at the start of the War, and swept back with the sides in short curls. If the hair was long behind, it could be worn in a chignon or held neatly in a snood.

Veronica Lake, an American actress and film star, popularized a style of hair fashion for a brief while. Known as the Veronica Lake style, it was shoulder length hair allowed to hang loose and falling slightly over one eye. This fashion was discouraged during the War years because of the danger of long loose hair near machinery.

By about 1941, very short hair became fashionable, mainly because it was more practical and easier to keep tidy, and it also lay better beneath the regulation hats and caps mainly worn in the factories. Hair was sometimes worn as short as 8 cm. Styles varied: some had side sweeping at the back or curls on the top or over the ears.

In 1942 hairstyles altered. The hair was worn high in the front, sometimes in curls on top from front to back and the remaining hair allowed to hang loosely below shoulder level at the back. By about 1946 upswept hairstyles were achieved by having the front hair in bunches or rolls of hair on top with the remainder allowed to hang down over the shoulders. Hair could also be worn in a bun on top of the head, extra fullness being obtained by inserting a round of false hair, with the real hair placed over to conceal it. Chignon styles could

Short practical hairstyle, c. 1942

Page boy style with the side hair swept up

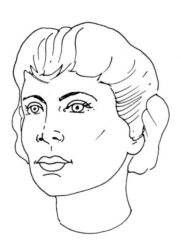

Various wartime hairstyles

Long hair curled under at the ends, c. 1946

also be created with the help of a false hair bun which could be made into an oval shape.

Towards the end of the 1940s fringes or 'bangs' (a longer fringe curled under) were also popular. The mass of the hair could be either long or short. Wavy hair was also popular.

By around 1950 short hair worn close to the head became fashionable, and an 'urchin' style also became extremely popular. This entailed the hair being cut unevenly and brushed so as to make it appear untidy. A 'bubble' cut hairstyle with the hair cut short all over and formed into curls, was also popular after the War, although fairly long hair from about 5 to 10 cm at the nape and 15 cm at the crown was worn by many.

Hair bleaching became very fashionable and many women bleached their own hair with special preparations that contained peroxide.

ACCESSORIES

Elegant gloves were less worn during the War as they were on coupons. However many hand-knitted gloves and mittens were worn for warmth. After the War long evening gloves were again worn, either in a soft leather such as kid or glacé kid or in the new nylon and synthetic materials made up in light semi-transparent lacy designs. The long gloves could be ruched and elasticated from the wrist up to the elbow or wherever they ended, to give a better fit.

Hairstyles of the 1939-45 period

Handbags were generally fairly flat and oblong in shape with strap handles, and on frames with clasp closures. During the War years handbags became more practical, and rather than just being used to contain purses and make-up, they became larger in order to hold ration books and identity cards. Some even had a compartment to carry a gas mask. Many bags had adjustable handles or straps so that they could be lengthened and worn over the shoulders. Large bags remained in fashion after the War and were made in various styles and shapes. Although felts and other fabrics had been used extensively during the War, leather was also much in use until plastics began to make their appearance. Evening bags, as always, remained smaller and more ornate than those in everyday use.

1938-39

Fur stoles were worn only for evening wear, although fur trimmings on coat collars and cuffs were still occasionally to be seen. Scarves were more popular and were made of silk, wool or rayon. They usually had a printed design. Square scarves were sometimes worn as headwear, and long scarves could be worn around the neck with one end longer than the other and tucked into a belt. Shorter or square scarves were draped and could be held in place in the front with an ornamental ring.

Shoes, stockings, scarves and even perfumes were marketed by the couture houses as fringe attractions to tempt the less wealthy, who although not able to afford the original garments, wanted to have something with a couture label. Dior offered a total look with shoes, bags and hats matching the dresses. Even his perfume was planned to match the ensemble of the wearer.

Short upswept hairstyle, c. 1949

Umbrellas were made in a great variety of colours and were also made collapsible so that they could be carried in the larger handbags.

Belts, often wide, could be made of an elasticated material. During the shortage of leather, scraps were cut and interlinked to make belts, a variety of colours being used to give a bright and cheerful appearance.

A great deal of chunky imitation jewellery was worn. Earrings fastened with clips at the back made the wearing of these a more popular and usual addition to everyday jewellery. Many earrings were large and made in coloured plastic materials; they were especially fashionable with the shorter hairstyles.

Hairstyle, c. 1946

The ever growing demand for make-up in the 1930s encouraged manufacturers to produce greater varieties of colours in both lipsticks and face powders. Face powders were often perfumed as well. Cream rouge was also much in vogue to colour the cheeks.

Perfumes, which had been too expensive for ordinary people, being mainly imported from France, were later bottled in smaller containers, thus reducing the price per bottle.

Eyeshadows matched the colour of the eyes, and gold and silver tints were poular for evening wear. Mascara was used for tinting eyelashes, and blue-green was considered to be a flattering colour. False eyelashes could be added to give extra length. Eyebrow pencils could also be used to accentuate the eyes. Lipsticks, apart from being in a variety of reds, were also made with a shiny finish. Nail varnish in deep vivid shades of red was used not only on fingernails, but on toe-nails as well, especially when open-toed sandals were worn.

'Stockingless cream' was devised, which was a cream dye the colour of sheer silk stockings which were in very short supply. This was painted on to the legs, and a 'seam' then painted down the centre back with an eyebrow pencil.

The War curtailed the supply of make-up as many of the essential ingredients were required for War purposes. When wartime restrictions ended the variety of make-up and skin preparations increased immensely. Cosmetic sales depended heavily on advertising and clever packaging and lipsticks were produced in thin versions as 'lipline pencils' to enable better lines to be drawn, and then filled in with the conventional lipstick. An emphasis on glamour came about with the greater freedom and the film star image which exerted a great influence. Peroxide hair bleaches were very evident when film stars had fashionable blonde hair.

Long embroidered evening glove, c. 1940, and short kid glove, c. 1940

Children

Children's fashions altered very little from the previous period during the War years.

School uniforms still consisted of gym slips and blouses for girls and shirts and shorts for boys. School hats and caps were worn, although girls were permitted to wear school berets with the school badge displayed on the front. The badge also appeared on blazer breast pockets, hatbands and caps. V necked pullovers with either long or short sleeves were worn by both boys and girls for extra warmth in the winter.

Hoods were worn in the winter for warmth by girls and small boys. These were either knitted or of a warm fleecy material, and were sometimes known as pixie hoods. They often had a scarf attached which was practical both for keeping the hood on and for extra protection. Berets were also popular for girls, and these could also be crocheted.

Many children's shoes and sandals were round toed and had ankle straps to hold them on. Ankle boots were also popular for very young children to give extra support to the ankles. Socks could be either short or knee length and were made in a variety of colours.

Girls' party dresses invariably had short puffed sleeves, and most dresses ended just above the knees.

Pinafore dresses were a practical addition in the War years. Outgrown or old dresses could be converted by cutting off the sleeves and lowering the neckline if necessary; they could then be worn over a jersey or blouse or even another dress. Pinafore dresses could also be made of sheets, tablecloths or anything that was available. They were very useful for either covering up shabby dresses or protecting party dresses.

Tartan trews or slacks were worn by children to keep them warm in winter, and small siren suits were also available in the War.

Toddlers wore romper suits. These were made in much the same way as pinafore dresses, but buttoned together at the crotch.

Child's pinafore dress worn over a dress with short puffed sleeves

Child's coat with a pixie hood and short wellington boots

64

Glossary

Ascot Tie	Double knotted cravat with the ends held down with a scarf pin.
Bang	Fringe of hair curled, covering the forehead.
Basque	Continuation of upper part of a garment that forms a short skirt, flaps or tails from the waist down.
Batswing Sleeves	Sleeves cut to fit an armhole from shoulder to waist and ending in a small cuff or wristband.
Beret	Simple headwear made of a round piece of material gathered to fit the head.
Bishop Sleeve	Sleeve flaring out from the shoulder, the fullness gathered on to a band at the wrist.
Bolero	Short jacket ending well above the waistline with or without sleeves and always worn open.
Bouffant	'Puffed' — as applied to hairstyles and full-skirted dress styles.
Bowler Hat	Stiff round hat with medium-high crown and a curled brim.
Bow Tie	Small tie tied with two loops, the two short ends worn horizontally.
Brassière	Undergarment originally designed by Paul Poiret to lift and hold up the breasts.
Bush Jacket	Traditional safari jacket made of a water repellent material, belted and with four patch pockets.
Button Stand	Separate piece of material sewn to the front of an opening to carry buttons and buttonholes.
Cape	Sleeveless outer garment cut circular or flared.
Chesterfield	Popular overcoat, generally fitted, named after Lord Chesterfield.
Chignon	Fold or knot of hair usually worn at the nape of the neck.
Coat Dress	Dress fastening all the way down the front.
Coatee	Short coat or jacket.
Corset	Undergarment lightly boned or elasticated to support the figure in a fashionable contour.
Cowl Collar	Draped collar with folds.
Crepe	Crimped synthetic or real rubber used for soles and heels of shoes.

Crew Cut	Short hair, the top standing up like bristles, originally worn by university crews.
Crew Neck	Flat round high neckline.
Cross Pocket	Pocket set below waistline in the front with almost horizontal sloping opening.
Décolletage	Low cut neckline, often leaving the shoulders bare.
Dicky	Tucked or pleated or embroidered fill-in for a low décolletage.
Dinner Jacket	Jacket like a dress jacket without tails, cut similarly to a lounge jacket.
Dirndl Skirt	Full straight-cut skirt gathered at the waist.
Divided Skirt	Garment similar to long shorts, but pleated to hide the split.
Dolman Sleeve	Sleeve wide from the shoulder, similar to bishop sleeves, but shaped to the wrist.
Double-breasted	Overlapping front of jacket, coat or waistcoat with a double row of buttons.
Drainpipe Trousers	Very narrow trousers.
Drip-dry	Material that can be washed and dried without the need for ironing.
Duffle Coat	Short coat made of a thick material.
Dungarees	Workman-like overalls.
Edwardian Look	(F) Hourglass silhouette (M) long, narrow fitted suits.
Epaulette	Shoulder decoration.
Fichu	Softly draped collar of a lightweight material.
Flies	Closure concealing buttons and zip fastenings.
Four-in-Hand	Long necktie, narrow around the neck but widening at the ends and tied with one end hanging lower than the other.
Fringe	Hair cut short and allowed to fall over the forehead.
Frock Coat	Coat with long skirts or tails joined at the waistline.
Galoshes	Waterproofed overshoes.
Gibus	Collapsible opera or evening hat.
GI Cut	See crew cut.
Halter Neckline	Neckline with front fairly high and tied behind the neck, leaving the back and shoulders bare.
Headscarf	Scarf worn over the head.
Hobble Skirt	Narrow skirt tapering towards the hemline.
Homburg Hat	Felt hat, originally from Homburg, with narrow stiff brim, dented crown and a hatband.
Hood	Head covering, usually with a peak at the back. Made of a warm material, it could be fur edged or lined.
Housecoat	Loose buttoned or zipped coat, either long or short, for at home wear.
Housegown	Gown worn mainly in the mornings or evenings for house-work or relaxing. Made of simple materials and fastening down the front.
Inverted Pleat	Box pleats in reverse.

66

Ivy League Cut	Hairstyle similar to a crew cut, but the top slightly longer and more tousled.
Jabot	Lace or embroidered trimming worn at neck opening.
Jerkin	Sleeveless and collarless jacket.
Jetting	Piping or binding with self material.
Jodhpurs	Type of riding breeches full to the knee then tight to the ankle and held down with a strap under the foot.
Kerchief	Head covering.
Kick Pleat	Short inverted pleat at the base of the back or side of a tight skirt.
Kimono Sleeve	Sleeve wide at the armhole and cut in one with the garment.
Lapel	Folded back part of the front of a coat or jacket.
Lastex	Yarn wound around a rubber core, making a garment stretchable.
Lounge Jacket	Jacket without a waistseam.
Lumber Jacket	Straight unbelted short jacket made of a water repellent material and closed with a zip.
Mackintosh	Waterproof coat originally of a rubberized material.
Magyar Sleeve	Sleeve cut in one with the body of the garment, making a deep armhole.
Morning Coat	See frock coat.
New Look	Fashion innovation by Christian Dior in 1947. Small waistline and bouffant skirt.
Norfolk Jacket	Belted and pleated front and back.
Nylon	Completely synthetic material first used for stockings with which the name became synonymous.
Pants	Undergarment with elasticated waist, just covering the thighs.
Patch Pocket	Pocket made of the same material as the garment and sewn on to it.
Peep-toe Shoes	Shoes with the tip of the toe piece cut away to expose the toes.
Peg-top Trousers	Trousers cut full around the hips, narrowing towards the ankles.
Pencil Skirt	Straight slim skirt.
Peplum	Short flounce or overskirt from the waist of a bodice.
Peter Pan Collar	Small rounded collar.
Petticoat	Underskirt, see slip.
Pillbox Hat	Small round hat of stiffened fabric, made like a pillbox.
Pinafore Dress	Sleeveless dress, worn over a blouse or skirt and generally buttoned at the back.
Placket	Opening to facilitate getting into a garment, usually with a concealed fastening.
Platform Soles	Thick soles, thus raising the heels also.
Playsuit	Top and shorts in one, worn on the beach for play and sun bathing.

Plus-fours	Baggy breeches gathered at the knees by a band and buckle, reaching four inches (10 cm) below the knees.
Polo Shirt	Summer shirt with a round neck or small Peter Pan collar, pulled on over the head without any fastening.
Pork Pie Hat	Low-crowned felt hat with a crease in the crown.
Princess Style	Close fitting to the waist and then gored or flared to the hemline.
Pullover	Top garment without any front or back opening, worn by slipping over the head.
Quarters	Part of shoe supporting the side of the foot from heel to vamp.
Raglan	Sleeve devised by Lord Raglan; seams run from underarm to neck without a shoulder seam to allow for greater movement.
Raincoat	Water repellent overcoat.
Revers	Turned-back edge of a coat or waistcoat.
Roll Collar	Long collar without a point, merging into the garment.
Sailor Collar	Collar square at the back, narrowing to a V in the front.
Sheath Dress	Tubular and close fitting dress.
Shift Dress	Straight dress, smocked at the shoulders for extra fullness.
Shirring	Close parallel rows of stitching drawn to gather up the material.
Shirtwaister	Dress like a shirt, buttoned to the waist with a straight or flared skirt.
Shorts	Type of short trousers worn casually for sports wear.
Single-breasted	Closed by a single row of buttons and buttonholes.
Siren Suit	One piece overall-type suit worn mainly during the War years.
Skull Cap	Flat and round hat, fitting close to the head.
Slacks	Casual trousers worn by both men and women.
Sling-backs	Shoes with enclosed front but held on at the back only by a strap.
Slip	Fitted undergarment with a shaped bosom, the skirt cut on a bias, with narrow shoulder-straps.
Slipover	See pullover.
Sloppy Joe	Loose-fitting woollen pullover or cardigan worn over a shirt with the shirt collar showing at the neck.
Smoking Jacket	Jacket, generally of velvet or rich brocade decorated with braiding, made like a lounge jacket.
Snap Brim Hat	Soft felt hat with pulled-down brim.
Snood	Coarse hairnet or fabric bag to hold the hair loosely at the back.
Sou'wester	Hat based on a seaman's waterproof hat with a wide slanting brim, longer at the back than the front.
Spats	Short gaiters covering upper part of foot and ankle and fastened with buttons down one side.
Stepped Collar	Collar and lapel meeting with a notch between.

Stockingette	Close-woven elastic or stretchy material.
Suit	(F) Coat or jacket and matching skirt (M) Short coat or jacket and trousers and sometimes a waistcoat.
Sun Dress	Backless dress, mainly worn for sunbathing.
Sunray Pleats	Machine pleating radiating from the waist, becoming wider at the hem.
Suspender Belt	Belt with loops and buttons to hold up stockings.
Swagger Coat	Loose coat, flared from shoulder to hem.
Tail Coat	Coat similar to a frock coat, but with cut-away fronts.
Tailored Suit	Costume composed of jacket and skirt, mannish in style.
Teagown	Full length casual gown, usually quite ornate.
Tent Coat	Coat with a low standing collar, tent like in shape.
Tiara	Jewelled crescent-shaped headdress worn with formal evening wear.
Toggles	Wooden pegs held in place with a cord and pushed through a loop for a simple fastening, especially on duffle coats.
Top Hat	Tall silk hat.
Toque	Small close-fitting hat without a brim.
Trench Coat	Belted top coat, usually of gaberdine with Raglan sleeves or shoulder epaulettes, or a double cape to protect the shoulders.
Trouser Suit	Jacket and trouser ensemble.
Tucking	Folds of material sewn down.
Tulip Skirt	Skirt made of four overlapping curved parts.
Tunic Dress	Bloused bodice buttoning behind, worn over a skirt.
Turn-ups	The base of trousers turned up.
Twin Set	Matching jumper and cardigan.
Ulster Coat	Heavy loose-fitting coat with a whole or half belt at the back.
Urchin Hairstyle	Irregularly cut short hair brushed forward.
Utility Suit	Standard economically made lounge suit worn during the War.
Vent	Vertical slit from the hem up.
Vest	Undergarment worn for extra warmth.
Waistcoat	Short sleeveless jacket worn over a shirt.
Wedges	Heels and soles in one, flat on the ground.
Wellington Boots	Heavy waterproof boots reaching mid calf.
Welt	Folded piece of material sewn to an edge for strengthening or trimming.
Windcheater	Sports jacket made wind-resistant.
Wing Collar	Stiff standing collar with pointed turned-back tabs.
Wrap-over Style	Skirt in one piece crossing over and fastened in the front with ties allowing for an adjustable waist.
Yoke	Top part of garment sewn to lower part.

Select Bibliography

Amphlett, Hilda, *Hats*, Richard Sadler 1974

Arnold, Janet, *Handbook of Costume*, Macmillan 1973; *Patterns of Fashion* Vol 2, Macmillan 1972

Asser, Joyce, *Historic Hairdressing*, Pitman 1966

Bennett-England, Rodney, *Dress Optional*, Peter Owen 1967

Boucher, F., *20,000 Years of Fashion*, Abrams

Bradfield, N., *Historical Costumes of England*, Harrap 1972

Bradley, C., *History of World Costume*, Peter Owen 1955

Braun-Ronsdorf, M., *The Wheel of Fashion*, Thames and Hudson 1964

Brogden, J., *Fashion Design*, Studio Vista 1971

Brooke, Iris, *Footwear,* Pitman 1972; *English Costume 1900-1950*, Methuen 1951; *History of English Costume*, Methuen 1972

Carter, Ernestine, *Twentieth-Century Fashion*, Eyre Methuen 1975

Contini, M., *Fashion from Ancient Egypt to the Present Day*, Hamlyn 1967

Cooke, P.C., *English Costume*, Gallery Press 1968

Courtais, G. de, *Women's Headdress and Hairstyles*, Batsford 1971

Cunnington, C.W. and P.E., *English Women's Clothing in the Present Century*, Faber 1952

Cunnington, P. & Mansfield, A., *Handbook of English Costume in the Twentieth Century*, Faber and Faber 1970

Davenport, M., *The Book of Costume*, Bonanza 1968

DeAnfrasio, Charles & Roger, *History of Hair*, Bonanza 1970

Dorner, Jane, *Fashion,* Octopus 1974. *Fashion in the Forties and Fifties*, Ian Allan 1975

Garland, Madge, *History of Fashion*, Orbis 1975; *Fashion*, Penguin 1962

Gunn, Fenja, *The Artificial Face*, David and Charles 1973

Hansen, H., *Costume Cavalcade*, Methuen 1956

Harrison, Molly, *Hairstyles and Hairdressing*, Ward Lock 1968

Hartnell, Norman, *Silver and Gold*, Evans 1958

Laver, James, *Concise History of Costume*, Thames and Hudson 1963

Moore, D., *Fashion through Fashion Plates*, 1771-1970, Ward Lock 1971

Peacock, J., *Fashion Sketchbook 1920-1960*, Thames and Hudson 1977

Pistolese & Horstig, *History of Fashions*, Wiley 1970

Robinson, J., *Fashion in the Forties*, Acadamy/St Martins 1976

Saint-Laurent, Cecil, *History of Ladies' Underwear*, Michael Joseph 1968

Schofield, Angela, *Clothes in History*, Wayland 1974

Selbie, R., *Anatomy of Costume*, Mills and Boon 1977

Streatfield, Noel, *Shoes*, Franklin Watts 1971

Taylor, J., *It's a Small, Medium and Outsize World*, Hugh Evelyn 1966

Wilcox, R.T., *Dictionary of Costume*, Batsford 1970; *The Mode in Costume*, Scribner's 1948; *The Mode in Hats and Headdress*, Scribner's 1948

Wilson, E., *History of Shoe Fashions*, Pitman 1969

Yarwood D., *English Costume from the Second Century BC to the Present Day*, Batsford 1975; *Outline of English Costume*, Batsford 1967

Pictoral Encyclopedia of Fashion, Hamlyn 1968

Index

Accessories 24, 27, 61
Anorak 22

Badge 9, 21, 64
Basque 34, 38, 41
Bathing costume 22
Battledress 10
Beard 23
Beauty aids 63
Belt 15, 17, 20, 28, 31, 33, 34, 35, 37, 38, 40, 41, 44, 45, 47, 51, 52, 62; half 16, 17, 19; Swiss 31, 40
Beret 57
Blazer 19, 20, 21, 22, 64
Blouse 6, 28, 34, 35, 39, 40, 41, 42, 45, 46, 47, 64; tunic 6, 34
Bodice 8, 31, 33, 37, 41, 42, 44, 45, 51
Bolero 33, 34, 38, 39, 41, 42, 46, 47
Boots 21, 22, 23, 53, 64; elastic sided 22; riding 21; Wellington 23
Bra and pants 47
Brassiere 49, 50
Breeches 21, 47; riding 21
Briefs 49

Buckle 51, 52, 54
Bustle effect 31, 38, 42
Button 6, 10, 12, 14, 15, 16, 17, 19, 21, 25, 28, 34, 37, 38, 39, 42, 44, 47, 64; -brace 22; -hole 10, 14, 15, 17, 19, 25, 34; -stand 10, 21

CC41 6, 27
Cap 21, 24, 49, 57, 59, 64
Cape 51, 52
Cardigan 20, 21, 37, 39
Chignon 56, 60
Cigarette case 25; lighter 25
Clogs 55
Coat 6, 22, 28, 34, 37, 38, 51, 52; box 51; -dress 42; evening 44; swagger 51, 52; tent 52; Chesterfield 16, 17
Collar 6, 10, 14, 16, 17, 18, 19, 20, 21, 28, 31, 33, 34, 35, 37, 38, 39, 41, 42, 47, 49, 51, 52, 62; cowl 34, 35 37, 39, 41, 42; detachable 16; Peter Pan 39; point 16, 35, 52; roll 18, 19, 20, 39, 52; round 34, 35, 38, 39; shawl 18, 52; soft 16, 18; stand-fall

16; stepped 38; turned down 34, 37, 47; wing 16
Corselet 31, 33
Corset 50
Costume 37, 38, 40
Cuff 10, 17, 20, 22, 25, 37, 41, 47, 51, 52, 62; button 12; link 25; slit 10, 12, 14

Dandy 6
Dickie 37, 38
Drainpipes 6, 14, 15
Drapery 33, 42, 44
Drapes 6, 9, 12, 19
Dress 6, 8, 27, 33, 34, 39, 40, 41, 42, 45, 47, 49, 64; coat 18, 19, 37; cocktail 44; day 28, 31, 33, 44, 46; dinner 42, 44; evening 41, 44; jacket 35, 37; mourning 44, petticoat 28; pinafore 28, 46, 64; sheath 28; shift 28; tailored 31; tunic 34; two-piece 34; wedding 42, 44
Duffle 17
Dungaree 37, 45

Earrings 62
Edwardian look 6, 9, 14, 15, 23
Ensemble 34
Epaulettes 51
Evening dress 8, 28
Evening wear 18, 19, 41, 42, 44, 62
Eye shadow 63

Face powder 28, 63
Flaps 12, 14, 15, 37
Fly 15, 16, 17
Footwear 21, 22, 52, 55
Formal wear 18, 19, 41
Frock coat 10, 12, 14, 15, 21
Frogging 20

Galoshes 23
Gloves 19, 24, 25, 49, 61

Hair 6, 23, 45, 56, 60, 61; bleach 61, 63;
    bubble 61; crew cut 23; false 60, 61;
    Feather crew 23; G.I. 23; Ivy League
    23; net 56; urchin 61
Hairstyle 23, 28, 62
Handbag 62
Handkerchief 18, 19, 25
Hat 6, 19, 21, 22, 23, 57, 58, 59, 64;
    Breton 58; -band 64; bowler 21, 24;
    cloche 58; deerstalker 21; Eden 24;
    felt 21; Gibus 24; Homburg 24; pork
    pie 24; pillbox 57, 58; sailor 56, 58;
    snap brim 24; straw 58; top 10, 24;
    Trilby 24, 58
Headdress 6, 44
Headscarf 45, 56
Headwear 21, 23, 42, 56, 57, 62
Hobble 33, 37
Hood 5, 17, 45, 51, 52, 64
Hook and bar 15
Housecoat 44

Informal wear 10, 19, 44

Jabot 41
Jacket 6, 9, 12, 14, 18, 19, 20, 21, 22,
    28, 33, 34, 35, 37, 38, 39, 40, 41,
    45, 46, 47, 49, 52; bush 22; dinner
    16, 18, 19; fur 52; backing 21;
    lounge 15, 18, 21; lumber 21, 39;
    Norfolk 19, 22; riding 21, 47;
    smoking 21; sports 9, 19, 20; suit 40
Jeans 40
Jerkin 35
Jersey 64
Jewellery 62
Jodhpurs 21, 49
Jumper 35, 37, 39, 40, 46, 47, 49

Kerchief 56
Key ring 25
Knitwear 20, 21, 24, 39, 46, 61, 64

Lapel 6, 10, 14, 18, 19, 34, 37, 38;
    notched 19; roll 10, 14
Legwear 15
Lingerie 35, 50
Lipstick 28, 63

Loop 15, 20; and button 20

Mackintosh 17
Make-up 27, 62, 63
Mascara 63
Mittens 61
Morning coat 10, 12, 14, 15, 16, 19, 21
Moustache 23

Nail varnish 28, 63
New Look 5, 8, 28, 31, 38, 46, 49, 57
Nylon 8, 10, 17, 23, 28, 50, 52, 53, 61

Outdoor wear 16, 51
Overskirt 33, 38, 42
Overtunic 40

Panels 33, 41, 42
Peg-top 15
Peplum 31, 33, 34
Perfume 62, 63
Petticoat 49
Placket 33, 35
Playsuit 47,
Pleat 6, 9, 10, 19, 28, 31, 33, 34, 35, 37,
    38, 39, 41, 45, 46, 47, 51; accordion
    33; back 10; inverted 31, 33, 38, 47;
    kick 31; knife 38; sunray 46
Plimsole 21
Plus-fours 20, 21, 22, 23
Pocket 6, 10, 12, 14, 15, 16, 17, 20, 31,
    33, 34, 35, 37, 38, 40, 44, 52; breast
    12, 14, 17, 18, 19, 21, 25, 34, 64;
    cross 15; flapped 17, 18; fob 15; hip
    12, 14, 18; patch 9, 17, 20, 37, 45, 51;
    sham 31; side 12; slit 38, 51; ticket 14
Press stud 33, 44, 45, 46
Pullover 12, 20, 21, 22, 47, 49, 64

Raincoat 17, 52
Rever 33, 34, 39, 47, 51
Romper suit 64

Sandal 21, 23, 54, 55, 64
Sash 28, 35, 44
Scarf 16, 25, 49, 56, 59, 62, 64
Separates 40
Shirring 31, 33, 41
Shirt 9, 10, 16, 18, 20, 21, 22, 35, 49,
    64; boiled 18; nylon 21; waister 28,
    37
Shoes 6, 9, 15, 21, 22, 23, 25, 40, 49,
    53, 54, 55, 62, 64; ankle-strap 54,
    55; backless 54; brogue 21, 22, 53;
    court 54, 55; evening 55; ghillie 53;
    moccasin 53; peep-toe 53, 54; sling-
    back 53, 54, 55; sports 55; wedge 49,
    53, 54, 55
Shorts 21, 22, 40, 64; Tennis 47
Side slit 21, 42
Skirt 6, 8, 18, 21, 28, 31, 33, 34, 35,
    37, 39, 40, 41, 42, 44, 45, 46, 47,
    49, 51; bouffant 42; dirndl 33, 40;
    divided 40, 47; evening 41; maternity
    45; pencil 37; tennis 46; tulip 42
Slacks 28, 35, 44
Sleeves 8, 10, 17, 18, 20, 21, 22, 33, 35,

39, 41, 44, 45, 51, 52; batswing 31;
    bishop 37, 41, 42, 44, 51, 52; cap 41;
    dolman 8, 37, 39, 51, 52; kimono 37,
    38, 41; Magyar 35, 37; raglan 17, 35,
    39, 41; set-in 17
Slip 49
Slipover 20
Smock 45
Snood 45, 56, 60
Socks 22, 23, 49, 52, 64
Spats 19, 25
Sportswear 19, 20, 47
Strap 14, 15 16, 17, 23, 25, 41, 44, 47,
    62; and buckle 25
Stiffener 16
Stockings 6, 23, 44, 50, 52, 53, 62, 63
Stole 62
Suspender 23, 50; belt 49, 50
Suit 5, 6, 8, 9, 14, 35, 37, 38, 39, 40,
    44, 59; cardigan 39; demob 14;
    dinner 19; dress 25; jacket 37;
    lounge 9, 10, 12, 19, 21; palm beach
    22; siren 5, 9, 37, 45, 64; town 35
Swimming trunks 22; costume 47

Tab 17
Tail coat 10, 18, 19
Teagown 44
Teddy boy 6, 14, 23
Tie 6, 9, 16, 19, 20; Ascot 16; batswing
    bow 18; bow 16, 18, 19; four-in-hand
    16; ready-made 16; tie-pin 16, 25
Toggle 17, 20
Toque 57
Trews 64
Trousers 6, 9, 10, 12, 15, 19, 20, 22, 34,
    40, 41, 45, 49; flannel 19, 20, 21, 22;
    suit 40
Tucks 31, 34
Turban 6, 57
Turn-ups 6, 12, 15, 19, 40
Twin sets 37, 39

Ulster 17
Umbrella 22, 25, 62
Underskirt 28, 45
Underwear 49, 50
Utility wear 5, 9, 12, 14, 27, 38

Veil 57
Vent 10, 17, 21; back 10, 17, 18; centre
    10
Vest 49

Waistband 15, 20, 21, 28, 33, 40
Waistcoat 6, 9, 10, 12, 14, 15, 18, 19, 21
Walking stick 19, 22, 25
Watch 25; pocket 25; wrist 25
Welt 12, 17
Windcheater 20, 21, 22, 39, 47
Wristband 37, 41

Yoke 17, 19, 33, 35, 41, 47, 51

Zip fastener 5, 15, 20, 21, 22, 33, 35 ,
    44, 47, 53